LAW AS CULTURE

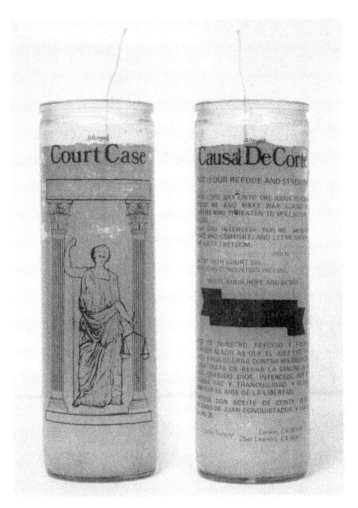

Candle used by Mexican Americans to ask divine intercession for a legal suit.

LAW AS CULTURE

An Invitation

Lawrence Rosen

Princeton Unversity Press

Princeton and Oxford

Copyright © 2006 by Princeton University Press
Published by Princeton University Press, 41 William
Street, Princeton, New Jersey 08540
In the United Kingdom: Princeton University Press,
6 Oxford Street, Woodstock, Oxfordshire OX20 1TW

Third printing, and first paperback printing, 2008
Paperback ISBN: 978-0-691-13644-8

The Library of Congress has cataloged the cloth edition
of this book as follows

   Rosen, Lawrence, 1941
   Law as culture : an invitation / Lawrence Rosen.
   p. cm.
   Includes bibliographical references and index.
   ISBN-13: 978–0-691–12555–8 (cl. : alk. paper)
   ISBN-10: 0–691–12555–4 (cl. : alk. paper)
   1. Culture and law. 2. Law and anthropology. I. Title.
   K487.C8R67 2006
   340′.115—dc22   2005029409

British Library Cataloging-in-Publication Data is available

This book has been composed in ITC New Baskerville

Printed on acid-free paper. ∞

press.princeton.edu

Printed in the United States of America

10 9 8 7 6 5 4 3

For Leonard V. Kaplan
and Warren J. Archer

Lawyers, scholars, friends

Contents

Illustrations

Preface

> If you think that you can think about
> a thing, inextricably attached to
> something else, without thinking of
> the thing it is attached to, then you
> have a legal mind.
> —*Thomas R. Powell*

If, like Thomas Powell, you feel vaguely uncomfortable trying to slip the bonds that attach law and life, you may find that your "legal mind"—and not your legal mind alone—is already attuned to the major thrust of this book. For it is precisely in those attachments—not just to something else but to everything else—that one may find the point of departure for this brief invitation to viewing law as culture. Coming at such matters both as an anthropologist and as a lawyer, I can, of course, indulge myself in each discipline's distinctive conceit: the anthropologist's, that everything is grist for our mill, from the first quiver in the green slime to the apotheosis of the highest of high-court judgments; the lawyer's, that if you have the benefit of a legal education, there is no subject whose mysteries will utterly elude you. And when the two conceits are joined, one may shamelessly approach the reader with the offer of seeing connections that reveal and enrich the insights of both.

The present study is, therefore, an attempt to entice the reader into seeing law as constituted by culture, and culture (in no small way) by law. Indeed, it is to suggest that law is so deeply embedded in the particularities of each culture that carving it out as a separate domain and only later making note of its cultural connections distorts the nature of both law and culture. If one sees religion as solely about "ultimate values," rather than concrete designs for understanding and directing everyday life; if one sees economics as only about "the rational calculation of means to ends," rather than the relations among people as they circulate things to which they attribute meaning; or if one sees law as exclusively concerned with the rules that regulate disputes, rather than as a realm in which a society and its members envision themselves and their connections to one another—if, in short, one pulls life and its articulations apart without ever rejoining them through a unified view of the nature of culture, then the reification of our momentary view of how the world is composed will triumph over our need to understand it from afar. The law is indeed an excellent storehouse of stories. But even more, it is an inexhaustible resource for understanding how, in any given circumstance, we come to tell these stories about ourselves, in ways that build the very reality they must, in turn, address.

The events of life and law do not, therefore, exist in the abstract but in the concrete patterns of everyday experience. Even in relatively brief compass it is possible to demonstrate that seeking connections as they arise is indispensable. Our examples will, of necessity, be drawn from many times and places, but such instances are not marshaled in some vain attempt at ethnographic completeness or comprehensive system-building. Rather, the aim is to think systemically about law as culture and, in the process of drawing comparisons, to explore, both theoretically and circumstantially, the interrelations of any society's multiple domains. To do so is to enrich our practical applications of law just as it may enrich our understanding of legal philosophy, the politics of law, and the different roles that law may play in a seemingly more interdependent world. This book is, therefore, intended as an invitation: both a request to consider specific ways in which legal and cultural systems form part of a unity, and an enticement to exercise those additional insights that an orientation towards connections invariably produces.

Acknowledgments

For the past three decades I have taught courses on law and anthropology at Princeton University and Columbia Law School, where I hold appointments, and as a visitor at the law schools of Georgetown, Northwestern, the University of Pennsylvania, and the American Bar Foundation. On four occasions I have also directed, under the sponsorship of the National Endowment for the Humanities, a summer seminar on anthropology and law for college teachers. Many of the examples and insights drawn upon in this work come directly from the courses and conversations these experiences have afforded me. To the many students and colleagues who have thus helped me think through the relation of law to culture my debt is both heartfelt and incalculable.

Portions of this manuscript were developed while I was a fellow of Corpus Christi College, Cambridge, and Wolfson College, Oxford. To the masters and fellows of those colleges I am delighted to record my deepest appreciation. I am also grateful to Carol Greenhouse for reading an earlier version of this book and to Gabriela Drinovan for help with the illustrations.

The book is dedicated to Leonard V. Kaplan and Warren J. Archer, in endless gratitude for our endless conversations about law and life—and why they actually have something to do with one another.

LAW AS CULTURE

Introduction

The creation of legal meaning
takes place always through an
essentially cultural medium.
—*Robert Cover*

Parables of the Law

In the 1950s an Australian aboriginal man named
Muddarubba threw a spear and killed an aboriginal
woman when she called him by a name that refers to
male genitals. You may, the white judge told an all-
white jury, find the aboriginal defendant innocent. If,
however, you think that even by the standards of his
own group he should not have killed the woman, you
must find him guilty of murder. But if, notwithstanding
our own belief that such killing is wrong, you think that
what this man did was acceptable by the precepts of
his own group, you may find him guilty not of murder
but of the less serious offense of manslaughter. The
decision, he concluded, is up to you.

———————

Late in the Second World War, a German woman's neighbors told Nazi officials that she was making defeatist statements. The woman was accordingly sent to prison, from which she was released at the war's end. The woman then sued her neighbors. By denouncing her to the existing regime, she argued, the defendants had violated a provision in the law code, which long predated the Nazi era, that allows one to sue another for acting "against good morals" (*contra bonos mores*). Accordingly, she asked the court to exact some sanction on her neighbors for having subjected her to the Nazi imprisonment.

———————

A Japanese man was residing in New York City. He had lived in the United States on other occasions and was actually quite knowledgeable about American law. But, as he told a colleague, he always wondered which agency of government you were supposed to go to if no one in the apartment building would talk to you.

Coming to Law

The history of human beings begins before the history of being human—and with it begins a crucial aspect of how we might usefully think about law.

Since the 1920s, paleontologists have made a series of stunning discoveries and have drawn from them a no less stunning conclusion. It began when scientists discovered the remains of early hominids who were capable of making and using tools. Previously, scientists had assumed that such behavior could not occur before we were fully human. But as the evidence grew, two inferences became inescapable. First, the capacity to make tools was part of a larger process of establishing the categories of one's everyday experience and manipulating these categories through the symbols that make them manifest. Thus, organizing work groups along lines of kinship or gender or, eventually, being able to communicate emotions and commands through speech, were, like the fabrication of tools, critical to being able to successfully conceptualize and work one's world. Moreover, this categorizing capacity—the key feature of the concept of "culture"—was not something that happened *after* we became human but something that actually *preceded* our present speciation. Thus, the acquisition of the capacity for culture, through the selective advantage it offered, contributed enormously to our evolution into *homo sapiens.*

The conclusion that follows is of enormous significance: Human beings possess the capacity to create the categories of their own experience, and this capability, having largely replaced instinct, came before—and was instrumental in creating—the animal we have become.

Culture—this capacity for creating the categories of our experience—has, in the view that will be central to our concerns, several crucial ingredients. As a kind of categorizing imperative, cultural concepts traverse the numerous domains of our lives—economic, kinship, political, legal—binding them to one another. Moreover, by successfully stitching together these seemingly unconnected realms, collective experience appears to the members of a given culture to be not only logical and obvious but immanent and natural. This sense of orderliness operates at both a conceptual and a relational level, organizing our view of daily life as commonsensical and our ways of orienting our actions to others as systematic and workable. Features that may not seem to be linked are, therefore, crucially related to one another: Our ideas of time inform our understanding of kinship and contract, our concepts of causation are entwined with the categories of persons we encounter, the ways we imagine our bodies and our interior states affect the powers we ascribe to the state and to our gods. In short, we create our experience, knit together disparate ideas and actions, and in the process fabricate a world of meaning that appears to us as real.

Law is one of these cultural domains. Like the marketplace or the house of worship, the arrangement of space or the designation of familial roles, law may possess a distinctive history, terminology, and personnel.

But even where specialization is intense, law does not exist in isolation. To understand how a culture is put together and operates, therefore, one cannot fail to consider law; to consider law, one cannot fail to see it as part of culture.

The moment we approach law in this fashion—the moment we start to think in terms of connections—the questions we ask and the theories we apply reveal themselves as deeply intertwined. When Muddarubba reacted to the woman's utterance by throwing a spear at her, was he envisioning her use of that word as a challenge to his manhood—and with it his ability to provide for his dependents in a difficult environment? Or was it, like using an epithet to one's commanding officer, a challenge to the authority structure that has allowed the tribe as a whole to survive? What sense of the order of the world is set in play for Muddarubba—or, crucially, for the women in their society—by this utterance, and how can we translate the concepts through which their world is composed from one cultural and legal system to another? When the German woman sought relief for the moral wrong she said was done to her by neighbors, to whom did the court turn since, as they said, "good morals" should be gauged by the views of those members of society who are deemed "just and equitable"? Indeed, in what ways did that assessment partake as much of their commonsense assumptions about human nature and human relation-

ships as of the history of German legal thought? And
when the Japanese visitor found himself alone in a
strange country, what sort of response to his question
about the appropriate agency to help would have
made sense to him; what is it he thought that law, by
virtue of its capacity to summarize his experience,
should be able to do about his disturbing sense of
loneliness?

It is no mystery that law is part of culture, but it is
not uncommon for those who, by profession or context, are deeply involved in a given legal system to act
as if "The Law" is quite separable from other elements
of cultural life. Lord Mansfield could famously say
that the law "works itself pure," while Lon Fuller could
assert that since good is more logical than evil, the
result of the reduction of contradiction through common-law reasoning will necessarily be "to pull those
decisions toward goodness." And certainly believers in
a given religion may envision the precepts of its atten-
dant law as universally true. But context is crucial:
When we hear a court speak of "the conscience of the
community," "the reasonable man," or "the clear
meaning of the statute," when we watch judges grapple with parenthood as a natural or functional phenomenon, or listen to counsel debate whether surro-
gate motherhood or a frozen embryo should be
thought of in terms of "ownership," we know that the
meaning of these concepts will come not just from

the experience of legal officials or some inner propulsion of the law but from those broader assumptions,
reinforced across numerous domains, that characterize the culture of which law is a part. And when we
seek law outside of specialized institutions—when a
kinsman mediates a dispute or members of a settlement use gossip or an informal gathering to articulate their vision of society—the terms by which they
grasp their relationships and order them will necessarily be suffused by their implications in many inter-
connected domains.

In each instance, law is so inextricably entwined in
culture that, for all its specialized capabilities, it may,
indeed, best be seen not simply as a mechanism for
attending to disputes or enforcing decisions, not solely
as articulated rules or as evidence of differential power,
and not even as the reification of personal values or
superordinate beliefs, but as a framework for ordered
relationships, an orderliness that is itself dependent on
its attachment to all the other realms of its adherents'
lives. Different societies may play up one or another
institution as a vehicle for creating and exhibiting this
sense of order—whether it be in the elaborate rituals
of Bali or India, the theater of tragedy and comedy in
ancient Greece, or the drama of a British or American
trial—but nowhere is law (in this sense of ordered relationships) without its place within a system that gives
meaning to its people's life.

> Law doesn't just mop up, it defines. It doesn't just
> correct, it makes possible. What it defines, the
> meaning frames it sets forth, is an important force
> in shaping human behavior and giving it sense,
> lending it significance, point and direction. [We
> can view] law not so much as a device or mecha-
> nism to put things back on track, when they have
> run into trouble, but as itself a constructive ele-
> ment "within culture," a style of thought, which
> in conjunction with a lot of other things equally
> "within culture"—Islam, Buddhism, etc.—lays
> down the track in the first place.
> —Clifford Geertz

We can, therefore, approach a variety of legal systems looking for the ways in which, as part of their
larger cultures, each finds itself having to address certain common problems. Among these are the ways in
which social control is fabricated through a mix of "formal" and "informal" mechanisms, the ways in which
facts are created for purposes of addressing differences
and rendering the process of determining truth and
consequences consistent with common sense, the
means by which reasoning applied in one domain (like
the law) remains linked to the style of reasoning that
binds other elements of the culture together, and the
ways in which law may create a sense of an orderly universe well beyond its role in addressing whatever dis-

putes may arise. Seen in this fashion, some unusual features begin to present themselves, features that we will return to as we weave our way through a number of these common legal concerns. Three in particular are, however, worth noting at the outset.

Metaphor, Fact Creating, and Cosmology

The first has to do with the role of metaphor. This may seem a more appropriate subject for a book on literature than law, but metaphor may well be the key mechanism through which all of the crucial connections among cultural domains take place. To speak of one's body as a "temple," home as a "castle," intellectual life as "a marketplace of ideas," or equality as "a level playing field" is far more than mere wordplay: Such metaphors connect what we think we know with what we are trying to grasp, and thus unite, under each potent symbol, those diverse domains that must seem to cohere if life is to be rendered comprehensible. Indeed, if, as an aspect of our species' nature, thought is not intrinsic, closeted in some "secret grotto of the mind," but extrinsic, living in the publicly worked symbols that give it momentary materiality, then metaphors are central to the creation of thought and to binding diverse categories into a manageable whole. And even if the organization of our categories does not simply replicate the structure of our relations, the linkages—of style, identity, and strength—are integral to the capacity of people to orient their own thoughts and actions in terms of those they encounter. As we look for the telltale place of culture in law and the inescapable role of law as culture, we will necessarily have to consider the role of metaphor as a unifying agent.

[T]here is in cultures a strain toward conceptual consistency or logical integration, and in social systems a strain toward functional integration in the sense that normatively governed patterns of interaction complement each other. . . . Both "society" and "culture" are abstractions from the same phenomenon—social action. As [Gilbert] Ryle puts it, ". . . the styles and procedures of people's activities *are* the way their minds work and are not merely imperfect reflections of . . . the workings of minds." But the requirements of cultural consistency and functional integration are somewhat different. Putting one's thoughts in order and putting one's affairs in order are rather different activities for either a person or a community. They proceed along different lines, but tend to react upon one another so as to produce not a one-to-one matching of ideas and social relations, but rather a continuing process of mutual adjustment and challenge.
—Lloyd A. Fallers,
  Law without Precedent, 1969, 316

A related consideration is the way any society, or institution therein, creates facts. Again, this may seem an odd way of putting the matter. Why not say "discovers" the facts, or even "acknowledges" them? But if, as category-creating creatures, we are constantly forging the units of our own experience, then "facts," like anything else, must be fabricated, connected, rendered obvious. So, as we will see, the common law may have developed its form of reasoning in association with its culture's ways of viewing essential human nature, its ways of construing people's inner states as part of a particular religious history, and its rules of evidence in association with changing visions of economic and political "certainties." By contrast, the law of many Islamic or Asian cultures may turn on issues of moral equivalence or social hierarchy, each culture fashioning a baseline from which, out of the totality of sense and imagination, a believable way of grasping facts can be forged. If culture is by definition constitutive, so too must law be formative and not simply formed.

And third, while analyses of law tend to focus on conflict and resolution, rule-making or rule-applying, one can—without in any way downplaying these aspects— also see law as contributing to the formation of an entire cosmology, a way of envisioning and creating an orderly sense of the universe, one that arranges humanity, society, and ultimate beliefs into a scheme perceived as palpably real. Edward Levi once wrote that law "has absorbed within itself a view of the nature of

human beings, and of how their acts and the incidents
which overtake them may be classified for favor or penalty." He could have added that in doing so it reflects
and creates a still broader sense of the order of all
one's experience. We may, as Clifford Geertz suggests,
"conceive of law as a species of social imagination," not
just, or even primarily, as a vehicle for keeping society
functioning: Law, as part of that imagination, may help
us grasp the world in which (to use Annie Dillard's
phrasing) "we find ourselves so startlingly set down."
Thus to consider the styles of legal reasoning or the
structure of cultural assumptions built into many legal
precepts is to offer both a window into the larger culture and, no less importantly, to gain an often under-
valued window into legal processes themselves.

In the course of these pages, then, our focus will remain on the kinds of problems that face any legal system and how these issues move in tandem with the features of their broader cultures. The trick, of course, is
neither to engage in some quest for the universal nor
to approach each legal system as an exercise in butterfly collecting. Instead, it is to focus on connections, to
keep turning the kaleidoscope so that as different legal
and cultural systems appear we appreciate how differently they may arrange the connections among their
parts. In the process we will, necessarily, be attending
to the multifarious forms of cultural/legal integration
that only such comparison can make visible. We will
also be able to consider some of the legal and social

theories that have been central to Western jurisprudence in the light of a broader comparative framework. And throughout we will see how quite different orientations can reveal possibilities and relationships that are vital to the most practical as well as the most theoretical of legal concerns.

CHAPTER 1

Law and Social Control

> The law is an inexhaustible reservoir
> of good stories because it deals
> with humanity between the hammer
> and the anvil.
> —E. Lipsky

Conflict and Relationship

Two businessmen enter into a contract. Both are well
known to people in the trade and both have engaged
in similar contracts—perhaps even with one another—
over the course of time. Part way through the duration
of their contract, however, one of them fails to perform
as required. What options are open to the "injured"
party? What resources—legal, conceptual, relational—
may each draw upon to resolve a dispute, in what
order, and with what implications?

In a famous article published in 1963, Stewart Macaulay argued that American businessmen, faced with

such a situation, rarely sue for breach of contract. Even though they go to lawyers to draft the original agreement and the law is usually quite clear, they rarely bring a case to court. Was the contract, then, a wasted formality? As scholars have pointed out, a contract is more than the reduction to writing of mutual mistrust: Contracts clarify obligation, encourage negotiation, establish a working framework for voluntary agreement, aid memory, transmit group experience, and encourage a sense of seriousness. Nor is it simply the cost of litigation that dissuades people from suing for breach, even though cost certainly affects litigation prospects. For in addition, one has to look at the relationships of the parties within and beyond their own business community. To sue may well be to risk the loss of flexibility that may benefit all parties at different times, to undermine the informal mechanisms by which reputations are made and kept, and to disrupt ongoing relationships for momentary gain. Even if people have fewer cross-cutting attachments than at the time of Macaulay's original study and are less likely than they once were to contract with members of their own "club," bounded trade groups and business associates may still invoke informal pressures to avoid litigation. In even so "legalistic" an environment as contract law, therefore, it is the full array of social control mechanisms that informs the meaning and applicability of the law and the role it plays in the broader process of exchange.

Often businessmen do not feel they have "a contract"—rather they have "an order." They speak
of "canceling the order" rather than "breaching
our contract." . . . Most clients, in heavy industry
at least, believe that there is a right to cancel as
part of the buyer-seller relationship. There is a
widespread attitude that one can back out of any
deal within some very vague limits. Lawyers are
often surprised by this attitude.
—Quoted in Stewart Macaulay, "Non-Contractual
   Relations in Business," 61

The American response to disputes is hardly unique.
Studies of other societies show analogous considerations. Descriptions of Israeli communal settlements
suggest that where the ideology of collective ownership
was strong, "informal" mechanisms—particularly gossip and scandal—were effective in communicating and
enforcing acceptable behavior. Even so minor an intru-
sion as personal possession of a teapot could lead to
clique formation that had to be met with strong pressures lest the sense of the whole community as the irreducible unit of society be undermined. In the antebel-
lum American South, as among religiously oriented
groups in some regions today, the informal pressures
of public opinion—including the subtle power of
women to exert moral authority by socially isolating
those who violated accepted standards—may have out-

weighed apparently formal rules. Gossip, as various scholars have noted, is not mere backbiting: It articulates group standards, casts up group leaders, establishes collective boundaries, socializes newcomers to group history and traditions, and signifies personal inclusion. So divorced from individual creation may gossip appear and so strong its capacity to regulate conduct that the Greeks built temples to the god Rumor (Fama), whose epiphanies bespoke the unseen hand that orders social relations.

Distinctive legal institutions and informal mechanisms of social control fit with still other aspects of any culture. In many African and Native American groups, in-laws or siblings may be required to physically avoid one another, or jokes and salacious comments, rather than being privately relayed, must be publicly addressed to those kinsmen with whom conflict is seen as a real threat. On the surface these practices may appear simply as functional substitutes for dispute resolution, but as one looks more closely at their social and cultural involvement, other connections appear.

For example, among many Eskimo and Berber groups "song duels" were arranged between disputants. Characteristically, opposing parties and their supporters would face one another and hurl arguments, phrased with varying degrees of poetry and wit, at the opponent. The goal was to persuade those gathered of the justice of one's claims, public approval for the acts of one party or the other constituting the ultimate judgment. Closer inspection, however, reveals that while in some cases the "duels" do address disputes, in many instances what may be at work is the maintenance of the very ambiguity of social relations. Having learned since childhood that they should be allowed to do what they want so long as it does not elicit violence in others and that the human universe is radically unpredictable, Eskimos traditionally accorded one another a considerable amount of leeway in individual social arrangements. Eskimos of the central Arctic, like Berbers of the Atlas Mountains, thus retained the flexibility of negotiated ties to others by dramatizing tensions in such a way as to reassert their own capacity to maneuver. For them, song duels, with their magnified irony and barely masked antipathy, dramatized and preserved the ambiguous nature of all relationships—itself a process that may "resolve" the dispute. Indeed, as Hervé Varenne suggests, what may be shared in a culture are less discrete beliefs than the terms for *dis*agreement.

In other societies variants of the emphasis on flexible social relations may be deeply inscribed in legal practice. Comaroff and Roberts thus describe the customary law of the Tswana of South Africa as incorporating not a set of rules but an undifferentiated repertoire of norms that, far from removing ambiguity, lead to the "legitimization of competing constructions of reality in terms of which situational conflict is expressed."

Fig. 1. Zulu ordeal, 1931. (Original photo by Commander
A. Gatti, University of South Africa. Courtesy of Northwestern
Law School, Wigmore Collection.)

As people negotiate the public recognition of their relationships, flexibility and uncertainty are, as in the
conception of social life generally, inextricably united.
Thus, as one of the authors' Tswana informants said,
"reality is never what it seems; you think one thing and
find out it is another, and then another." The result,
however, is not chaos, but law that is only comprehensible as part of an entire array of mechanisms by which
characteristic qualities are teased out of each situation,
even as the particularities of each situation remain free
from implacably constraining restrictions.

> However much disputes and their settlement are
> conducted in a rhetoric of community values ap-
> pealing to something like *communitas*, what peo-
> ple learn from them is much more pragmatic in-
> formation: the limits of community tolerance for
> different kinds of behaviour under a variety of cir-
> cumstances, an appreciation of how particular in-
> dividuals respond to provocation, and some map-
> ping of the changing alliances that form the basis
> for daily interaction.
> —Elizabeth Colson, 1995

In each sociolegal system the fit with other elements
of the culture is crucial to the mechanism's effect: The
points of stress marked by joking relations usually connect with the lines of marital alliance and exchange,
while song duels may track economic ties or the ambiguous nature of relationship itself. Commonly, where
people have multiple, cross-cutting ties, the impact on
relationships brought about by a lawsuit, self-help, or
breaking off all ties will be muted by the interdepen-
dency formed across religious, kinship, and political
bonds. Tribesmen who must exchange across ecologi-
cal bounds, no less than Western businessmen who
want ongoing commercial relations—or who are involved in the same church or golf club or charity—may
all be made to feel the pressure to avoid an overt break.
These pressures may be public and intense or play on

an individual's own sense of self. Arbitration decisions in the American cotton industry, for example, do not list participants' names, but the gossip network is said to be so effective that few are willing to risk their reliability as trading partners by clearly violating group standards. At times various American magistrates have ordered the posting of public notices of an individual's criminal record or personal debts, prompting intense debate on the propriety of such shaming. In other instances, the focus is on a kind of enlightened self-control: Duke University's student honor code calls for no enforcement, appealing instead to one's "concept of honor," while the code at Mount Holyoke College speaks of the community as based on "an exchange of gifts" that has a profound effect on "the image one has of oneself." And the behavioral code at my own undergraduate college—which I should like to think was not without genuine content—consisted of just two words: "Be Discrete."

From the perspective of evolutionary and functionalist theory, even conflict may appear as socially and culturally integrative. Some ethologists thus claim that conflict in our nearest primate cousins correlates with higher rates of grooming and solidary behavior, thus suggesting that it is not the conflict that is adaptively advantageous but the socializing that follows it. Earlier, sociologists like Georg Simmel and Lewis Coser had argued that conflict intensifies in-group structures and identity, forges shared orientations, and acts as a safety valve for potentially more serious divisions. It can even be argued that conflict with outsiders has its advantages: The feud limits violence to tit-for-tat attacks rather than the war of all against all, and (as among the Arabs, for example) the legitimacy of a leader may depend in no small part on his acknowledgment by the group's enemies, thus reinforcing the norm that one does not utterly destroy the enemy but always leaves him a way out. Even the ancient principle of "an eye for an eye" may be seen not simply as a mark of retribution but as a structured limitation on potentially escalating violence. When one looks at legal disputes and cultural norms in the light of these theories, one can, again, see that dispute resolution may arguably be secondary to forces aimed at preserving a sense of orderliness and options for the future.

Law does not, therefore, depend on express sanctions or even the existence of an actual sovereign; nor does it require utter precision to possess content. The disjunction between formal contract law and actual relationships among businessmen, for example, may have far less to do with legal efficiencies or even the history of courts and lawyers than with the cultural ideas of the autonomous person, the image of human sociality, and the role of formal law in maintaining a sense of order even when the primary mechanisms of social control, in fact, lie elsewhere. It is not, as some claim, that "law cannot bear very much reality": It is that the reality of law is not self-proscribed, living in its own institutional context, working itself pure to its own rationale. Like every other aspect of a culture, law lives in a place that is not solely of its own making. As we open up the idea of law to intersect those other domains where we fabricate the categories of our everyday experience, we open up the possibility not just for an enlarged sense of how law draws upon all the other domains of life for its own ends: We also see how cultures embrace both the order law seeks and the openendedness that life requires to fashion a world that, for those who entangle their lives in its terms, gives order and flexibility to individuals and groups alike. An excellent place to see these processes at work is in the implementation of moral precepts in a context where some action must be taken.

Morals, Law, and Culture

The literature of law has long centered on the relation of law to morals, and the contributions of philosophers and jurists in every culture have highlighted the contested relations between these two domains. Although some have argued that law and morals should be kept distinct analytically, if not practically, it is crucial to address the issue of how, as part of the larger culture, moral precepts find their voice in different legal systems. By exploring several examples of how this process operates we can see some of the connections through which law and morals contribute to one another's very structure and meaning.

Among a group in the Philippines called the Tiruray it is believed that men are, by their very nature, disposed to violence. Accordingly, if a man feels some sense of injury, of being ill at ease, he must be attended to quite carefully. Within the society a number of individuals over the course of time have been recognized as possessing a refined sense of appropriate conduct as well as personal sensibility. When the injured party addresses himself to one of these respected figures, the latter consults with other knowledgeable men and, if they feel it appropriate, a collective hearing is arranged. The one who attends to a person's sense of injury must, therefore, balance the subjective sense of discomfort with the standards of the group as a whole. Lacking any enforcement powers but drawing on moral rules as the sole source of his guidance, the system's representative seeks a recognizable causal connection and a remedy that joins both the individual's felt sense of unease and the criteria by which legitimate support for his injured feelings may be publicly addressed. Because they do not believe that a simple assertion of right and wrong ever really ends a potential dispute, the Tiruray's focus is constantly on the delicate interplay of personal discomfort and moral principles that can express and momentarily articulate the bases for continued interaction. This style of legal-mindedness is, moreover, consonant with the way in which leadership, political influence, and personal repute are made manifest in the society in many other domains.

Such mechanisms thus have distinct boundaries, in their determination of what constitutes a "fact" as much as in the goals of any proceeding. Where distinctive legal institutions exist, the means for addressing these concerns may take quite varied forms. In his analysis of the Barotse of present-day Zambia, Max Gluckman discusses cases in which royal judges may, for example, impress upon a man that he should be more generous to the wife he is divorcing than the law requires while still acknowledging that as judges they have no power to force the man to be more forthcoming. However, during a break in proceedings, others may remind the husband that he has multiple ties to the members of the court—as kinsmen, village mates, and trade partners—and not infrequently the litigant succumbs to these related pressures. The party may then be praised by the court for being such a good man. Thus where the Tiruray have regularized a process through which experienced individuals may draw directly on the moral precepts of their community— precepts that include attention to the individual's sense of injury—Barotse judges are not allowed to have resort to moral principles alone. Instead, they may use their multiple ties to an individual to conduce proper role behavior, even though the formal limitations on their ability to impose their own moral sense is quite circumscribed. At issue, then, is the "constitutional" dispersal of power in each of these societies, a process that depends not on recourse to strict rules but on the maintenance of order through diverse social, economic, and psychological pressures.

Comparisons to the American situation are intriguing in this regard. In a famous case involving a Jehovah's Witness who had gone to the hospital with a bleeding ulcer, Judge Skelly Wright, after rushing to the hospital to personally interview the patient and her husband, overruled the lower court and allowed the doctors to administer a blood transfusion. He later said that, faced with a life-and-death decision, he had an "instinctive reaction," and he was therefore prompted to conclude his written opinion with the striking words, "I vote for life"—even though his decision clearly went against the formal tenets of the woman's religion. Unlike the Tiruray figure who, in H.L.A. Hart's terms, is expected to give direct implementation to the primary moral rules, American judges, like their British counterparts, are not supposed to bring their own moral values into their decisions. Nor may they, like the Barotse judge, play on their extrajudicial ties to the parties. Thus, in a case of naturalization, where the candidate had been found guilty in his home country of the "mercy killing" of his deformed child, Judge Learned Hand expressed the dilemma when he said of the court: "Left at large as we are, with-

out means of verifying our conclusion, and without authority to substitute our individual beliefs, the outcome must needs be tentative," but that he imagined
"as to legally administered euthanasia, we feel reasonably secure in holding that only a minority of virtuous
persons would deem the practice morally justifiable,
while it remains in private hands." Judge Jerome Frank
dissented, arguing that the standard was not "virtuous
persons" at large: "I incline to think the correct statutory test is the attitude of our ethical leaders," though
he was unable to specify precisely who these leaders
were. Unlike the German judge, who, as in the post-
Nazi case mentioned at the outset, is personally authorized to look for "good moral precepts," the common-law judge must find some other way of bringing
morality into his opinions if he chooses to do so. He
may try to avoid imposing his own morality—as, for
example, Justices Frankfurter and Blackmun did with
great poignancy when they went against their consciences in death penalty cases for the sake of uphold-
ing the law. If common-law judges are to reach out to
moral propositions, therefore, their views may have to
be couched indirectly—sometimes even hypocriti-
cally—or through a claim that they accord with such
deep, shared sentiments of society as to be almost invisible in the process. When they do so, it is important to
ask in what other ways such practices are licensed in
the culture: When is it appropriate to tell a "white lie"
or ignore an "open secret"; how can one fashion a bar-

gain with one's conscience through a key cultural category like "entitlement" ("I've worked hard so now I'm entitled . . .") or trump law with "fairness"? In each instance, the meaning of a legal system's style of implementing moral propositions is incomprehensible without seeing its reverberations in other cultural contexts.

Less formal means of social control may also be tested in American courts. Judge Miles Lord, for example, tried to convince the makers of a harmful birth control device, the Dalkon Shield, that, beyond the requirements of their formal settlement, the executives should act like good people and notify all of the women using such devices of their peril. Unable to force them to "do the right thing," Judge Lord castigated and cajoled, concluding his remarks to the executives in open court by saying: "I know you have hearts and souls and consciences. Beg forgiveness and mend your ways. And I just want to say I love you. I am not mad at you." The result, however, was not capitulation to the moral standards he asserted but a suit against Judge Lord himself—with each side represented by a former U.S. attorney general—charging that the judge had exceeded his powers by trying to shame the executives in public. Judge Lord's problem, of course, was that in American law if one is to slip moral propositions into legal proceedings, it must be done notwithstanding the absence of any direct authority to do so.

Thus an American judge may refuse to intervene in the domestic differences of a couple concerning the education of their child if no divorce is involved, expecting the family or other social pressures to address the problem. Or a panel of judges may, even in the face of a vague statute, claim they are not deciding morality when they determine if a fetus is a person for purposes of a man's assault on his pregnant girlfriend. But unlike those systems of law in which the courts are meant to serve as direct agents of moral implementation or state power, common-law judges may have to engage in a certain amount of acceptable indirection, or risk appearing as though they are trying to impose a personal vision of right action. While each such instance needs to be understood in terms of the distribution of powers and legal goals being asserted, one cannot grasp the full meaning of the process involved without seeing how law has constructed the situation even as it has itself been constructed by the culture of which it is a part. A judge may, as one German commented of his own system, shoot an arrow first and afterwards draw a target around it with the arrow in the bull's-eye. But the idea of the arrow and the target—its connections to ideas of direction, moving inertia, or human origination—must precede the act if the entire process is itself to possess any meaning. Judges and legal philosophers may imagine that they have total, almost blinding, vision of the correct answer, the approach that binds all elements into a elegant whole, but that sensibility may come far less from personal insight than from drawing diverse domains together so they appear to grant to the legal result the kind of coherence that is recognizable within their culture as a whole.

Law and Custom

Legal systems must have some way of attending to concepts, values, and remedies which, even if they are not explicitly included in the law's design, are indispensable to the law's legitimacy and its capacity to respond to change. The breach of contract between a buyer and a seller will serve as an example.

In the United States the legislation dealing with such agreements is largely embodied in the Uniform Commercial Code, one of whose provisions (§ 2-302) says that if a court finds a contractual clause to have been "unconscionable," the court may refuse to grant enforcement. Few American lawyers know that this provision was, in all likelihood, actually inspired by a practice of the Cheyenne Indians. Karl Llewellyn, the main author of the statute, had worked with anthropologist E. Adamson Hoebel on a study of precontact Cheyenne law and was struck by their provision of rules that seemed to be vague and yet were filled up with meaning as particular cases arose. Out of the "crucible of conflict" (as they called it) the authors pointed to a number of instances in which seemingly amorphous concepts relating, say, to violations of the collective hunt or impermissible "borrowing" of another's horse, were given concrete and innovative interpretation within the broad framework of the governing concept. Llewellyn modeled the unconscionability provision with a similar thought in mind—that even those who do not share a given trade can recognize that contractual terms could prove to be excessively one-sided, harsh, or contrary to regularities developed within their community, and that the statute should allow room for flexibility consistent with these practices.

But where does one go to fill "unconscionability" with content? We could make the decision turn on whether the deal was "fair," but that might just replace one unknown with another. We could refuse to change the agreement, short of some actual fraud, mistake, or duress, because so general a doctrine as unconscionability may appear paternalistic, an interference with responsible negotiation. Indeed, we could regard the whole idea as an artifact of the romanticism about the democratizing force of men of commerce that Llewellyn drew from his Germanic roots or his American involvement (as one commentator put it) as "part of a 1930s radical, collectivist milieu." We could try to map this concept directly onto actual commercial relations or try to use it as a vehicle for conducing some ideal of commercial behavior. Or we could think of it, for example, as being similar to the German constitution's protection of "human dignity," "honor," and "personality"—a way of connecting collective self-image and communal identity. If parties deal with one another regularly, should fairness or the custom in their trade take precedence over the actual agreement, or some generalized weighing of what facilitates or hinders a valued social relation? Should a poor person unable to purchase an object except at a confiscatory price be shielded by the unconscionability statute, and if so, what is the theory of freedom of contract, individual will, and the nature of society itself with which the law would be operating? Whatever course we choose certain assumptions are being contested under this legal rubric, whether it is the idea that people are basically free to exercise their own will or that, since we can never specify all the constraints from which one ought to be free, we should avoid direct interference with an individual's choices. And if, as some scholars claim, actual cases reveal no clearly shared principles of substantive contract law in the United States, is it because those principles are absent or is it that, far from producing vast uncertainty, social and conceptual factors yield sufficiently acceptable practices to allow ongoing relationships to take primacy over imagined rules? In any legal system, then, the articulation of a broad standard may, as Llewellyn posited, be infused with specific cultural content, whether from the confines of a distinct trade group or from the application of cultural assumptions that lend legitimacy and meaning to any decision.

As one looks at the equivalent of propositions like unconscionability in other cultures, one can readily see some of the broader cultural factors that render such generalized concepts capable of specificity. Similar provisions in other countries reflect local history and culture: Britain's laissez-faire approach to contract, which draws no clear distinction between someone who takes advantage of the deal and what the broader socioeconomic impact of permitting it may be, is still visible in the limited remedies available for contracts that seem to favor one party more than another. France uses contract law, for example, to give considerable emphasis to the maintenance of family patrimonies against dissipation by a testator. Postwar Germany, whose rules on unconscionability are more explicit than those in the United States, has taken a more protective state view when the differential of bargaining power or experience appears unfair. Local issues may also take on special significance: The Israeli Supreme Court found unconscionable the contractual requirement that only Hebrew dates may be used on a tombstone; French courts have sought to extend the nation's statutes outlawing Holocaust denial to instances involving the murder of Armenians in the early twentieth century or to the posting of advertisements on the Internet for the sale from abroad of Nazi memorabilia. Some American commentators refer to their own unconscionability statute as having "only symbolic impact, an occasional bow in the direction of our incoherent hearts desires." Since an unconscionability provision is also to be found in the Uniform Premarital Agreements Act (as it earlier had been in the Indian Claims Commission Act of 1946), courts in the United

States may have to decide if a change in circumstances warrants revision of the initial expectations of husband or wife, a position French contract law, by comparison, has largely rejected. Like so many other domains of law, unconscionability offers an insight into a whole realm of cultural and philosophical assumptions. It may be most valuable, then, to see legislation in each of these instances as lying at the nexus of law and culture—a telling indicator of how specialist and everyday assumptions interact, such that the meaning of each is not fully comprehensible without the other.

The unconscionability example may also pose one of the many ways in which law and custom are related. In commercial relations in communities that are either tight-knit or dominated by particular interests, obligations may be very uniform and recourse to shared expectations given authoritative application. The "mixed jury" of early England brought together merchants from a trader's home country with local people, and thus helped to move the jury from being grounded in the truth known to locals and towards the determination of facts by officials. The International Institute for Conflict Prevention and Resolution (CPR), which has signed up hundreds of corporations who agree to alternative mechanisms for resolving disputes, saved these companies over $150 million dollars in court costs and legal fees between 1990 and 1992 alone. Such arbitration may, however, come at a price: Case law is not developed, arbitrators profit from their business, collective claims go unaddressed, and mediation is not free of charge. It has also been noted that although diamond or grain merchants in the present day may be bound by their colleagues' understandings, they may still press the edges as new opportunities and ambitions intrude. Courts may develop standards for applying what lies beyond the existing statutes—whether it be the longevity of the practice or its social and economic value to the community—and may, as they have at different moments in history, even defer to tribunals of knowledgeable merchants or elders. Courts, like their constituents, often accept without further proof that past actions predict future conduct, or that social status correlates with appropriate levels of compensation or support. These may, of course, also be the very issues that are contested in court, as among members of the population, but that is only to suggest how central cultural assumptions are to any form of social action. Similarly, colonial powers and their successor states have often sought to codify custom even at the risk of reifying it or merely incorporating the views of those who exercise the greatest influence at that moment.

What is often missing, however, from analyses of law's relation to custom is the wider range of cultural forces that may affect their interaction in any given situation. In their study of Tswana law in southern Africa, for example, Comaroff and Roberts demonstrate that the scope of customary law often appears to outsiders as lacking in organization and consistency. But the absence of highly differentiated rules and customs may actually contribute to the negotiated relationships that allow flexibility within social situations. Process takes precedence over rules, and "the fallacy of the rule" (as Pierre Bourdieu has termed it) leads one to imagine that custom in such a case is more like legislation than a repertoire of possibilities. If, as Edmund Leach argued, one of the prime functions of law is to keep us from crossing existing social boundaries, custom reinvigorates both ambiguity and alternatives to the flow of power. In what Sally Falk Moore has called the "semiautonomous domains of law"—which can coincide with industries or territories, tribal units or university disciplinary boards—the ordering of law and local practice is far more dependent on the culture of the group involved than on the mere imposition of rules from a sovereign. When, therefore, some African states have written into their codes a provision that "customary law shall apply in any civil case where, regard being had to the nature of the case and the surrounding circumstances, it appears just and proper that it should apply" (to cite the example of Zimbabwe), we need to know the logic of repercussions that informs both the choice of this principle and the realities of its implementation. By comparison, the disenchantment with customary law that occurred in twelfth-century Europe was, as we shall see, connected with the rise of the cities, the uncertainties of social arrangements, and the "discovery of the individual"—all of which cast cus-

Fig. 2. Moroccan scribe in the marketplace, ca. 1930, prepares documents for a legal case. (*Morocco: A Country of Islam* [Casablanca: Éditions Maurice Bory, n.d.].)

tom in a new and less satisfying light. Seen in this way, the history of custom becomes part of the history of culture and not simply part of law.

A good example of the relation of law and custom to cultural practice may be found in Islamic law. Western scholars of the sacred law (*shariʿa*) usually ignore custom because it is not categorized as a source of law in Islam, focusing instead on those legal scholars who emphasized analogic reasoning, consensus, or the authorized collections of noteworthy sayings by the

Prophet Muhammad himself. Yet, interestingly, in every Muslim legal system there is also some local version of the proposition that custom may take precedence even over that which is in the sacred law: In the words of a characteristic formulation, "Whatever is dictated by custom is as if dictated by law." As we shall see in more detail later, Islamic law presses decision-making down to locally knowledgeable figures and draws local practice directly into its assessment of persons and events. If, then, we start to connect this approach to other aspects of Islamic (particularly Arab) cultures, some comprehension of the meaning of custom in law begins to present itself.

Briefly, in Arab culture one is constantly arranging relationships in a highly personalistic way: In social life, as in the view of humankind presented in sacred text, the focus is constantly on the consequences that the arrangement of social ties has for creating a community of believers and fending off potential chaos. To know a person is to know his local ways of forming ties to others and the most likely nature of his networks of indebtedness; to know how to address potential disputes is to know the ways in which people in a given locale or type of arrangement may be encouraged to use when negotiating their own relationships. Traditionally there was no appeal in Islamic law because no one could claim final certainty, and facts were largely a function of the credibility of witnesses, a credibility that itself came from these witnesses being so involved in webs of relationship that they would be loathe to risk their reliability through false oaths. Thus, to come full circle, custom is a kind of unmarked category; it runs through the whole of the legal system without having to be set out as a separate source of the law. Because Western scholars have operated mostly from a civil law baseline—in which custom is generally not recognized as law until it is formally drawn within the ambit of the law—the role of Islamic custom as an important informative factor in many proceedings has often escaped emphasis. Whether it is in the implementation of moral ideas or the incorporation of social relations generally, the understanding of Islamic law, like any other system, is thus inseparable from the expression and enactment of the categories that define and vitalize the culture at large.

Family Resemblance

Some analysts have tried to capture these variant aspects of legal systems within a specific taxonomy. Like biologists they have sought to show relationships and key indicators by grouping the different forms of law into specific typologies. But often the result has been misplaced. We can certainly speak of Anglo-American "common law" or Continental "civil law" as historical developments, but as types of law we may find their key features to be present in systems not otherwise thought to share identifying features with these taxonomic categories. Other commonly used categories, like "religious law" or "primitive law," have almost no analytic utility. The reason is that the criteria of inclusion may not point out important relations of structure or function: It would be rather like categorizing animals by the hair on their legs or the number of teeth in their mouths. Instead, if, like modern biologists, we see variation as central and forms as the result of processes rather than the manifestation of pure or deviant types, a rather different taxonomic foundation may be suggested. For what may be more akin to having a spine or an exoskeleton, in categorizing legal processes, are the ways in which power is distributed among various social institutions and the ways in which changing cultural conceptualizations are given authoritative recognition. Seen in this fashion, we may spot connections that previously escaped our notice, and even avoid reifying the dichotomy of "formal" and "informal" legal institutions.

Specifically, we might group legal systems into three broad categories: those that treat law as an arm of central governance and only recognize sociocultural practices as law when they have been incorporated within the centrally controlled system; those that distribute power widely among counterbalancing institutions and rely on low-level institutions to draw changing cultural practices within their purview; and those that seek to maintain the legitimacy of established practices as a vehicle for sustaining the traditional social structure itself. We can denominate these three as civil law, common law, and traditional legal orders—bearing constantly in mind that whatever analytic merit they possess lies in their capacity to reveal relations we had not previously seen, rather than in any claim to being fixed realities.

Once again the example of Islamic law is instructive here. Because of its attachment to a sacred tradition, many comparativists speak of Islamic law, along with Jewish, Hindu, and other text-based systems, under the category of "religious law." But reference to supernatural sanction is not the key indicator—power and culture are. To build useful categories we need to ask the two questions noted above: How is power distributed and how are local practices absorbed into each system? Thus Islamic law actually may better be thought of as a kind of common-law system: Fact-finding and decision-making are pressed down to a range of witnesses, local experts, and textual advisors, while local culture is brought within the ambit of the law through the direct implementation of custom and common practice by these same figures. One of the reasons, it may be suggested, that in such places as the Sudan, Pakistan, and postrevolutionary Iran the state has been unable to simply implement an invariant form of fundamentalist Islamic law may be that, as a type of common-law system, Islamic law is not an arm of the state and is deeply attached to changing local circumstance; hence any attempt to render it a simple instrument of the state is bound to be undercut by its actual implementation at the local level. Islamic fundamentalists, ironically, may have made a category mistake about their own religion's law.

Legal systems do, of course, borrow from one another, just as other forms of cultural borrowing occur, so the question may be posed: How much of the larger cultural context needs to be moved along with a legal feature for such a transplant to work? For example, in the 1920s several midwestern states in America adopted a Scandinavian model of conciliation that has long proved effective in some of those countries for avoiding formal court proceedings. Since many of the people in these states were themselves of Scandinavian origin and since several of the states went so far as to write into their constitutions the requirement that such conciliation be tried before certain lawsuits, it would seem the program had a good chance for success. In fact, it collapsed within a few years. While the reasons are somewhat unclear, it appears that the pressures of local members of the community on the parties to conciliate rather than litigate had not taken root as in Scandinavia, and that the increased individualism of American culture led people to be more willing to end relationships through litigation than grudgingly ignore certain disputes for the sake of ongoing association. Just as Islamic fundamentalists may have erred in imagining that Islamic law is a kind of civil law system instead of a common-law variant, so too the cultural rootedness of a legal borrowing may or may not work depending on the commonsense assumptions and cultural role of legal proceedings at least as much as any professed efficiencies.

Indeed, the meaning and success of various conciliation or mediation mechanisms may depend, like legal transplants, on their broader context. Several examples—of an African procedure said to track an effective psychological technique, a conciliation mechanism employed by a Jewish organization located in New York City, and the so-called educative model of the former Soviet Union—will help to illustrate the range of connections that may be operative.

Conciliation in Context

The Kpelle of Liberia are described by James Gibbs as employing a legal procedure that bears a striking similarity to the psychological style employed by many therapists. The disputants are brought together with other members of the village at the complainant's home. The gathering is presided over by a mediator chosen by the aggrieved party, usually a kinsman who also holds some office or is recognized as a knowledgeable elder. Proceedings begin with a common prayer— much as one might start a potentially divisive athletic contest with a symbolically unifying national anthem— followed by the plaintiff's arguments and mutual questioning by both parties and all present. Very wide license is given to the parties' statements, and listeners are careful not to display any adverse reaction to the speakers' claims. Should anyone interrupt inappropriately he must send for some rum for everyone to drink. The mediator and others present eventually point out the faults of both parties. Whoever is seen to be predominantly at fault is expected to apologize as a way of preserving the dignity of all present, to give a token gift to the other party, and to present some beer to the mediator that is shared all around.

Gibbs argues that this style of proceeding is very similar to the four-part technique used by many psychotherapists: First, one demonstrates by the nature of the meeting itself support for the parties' concerns; second, one allows unbridled expression to those involved so they can get things off their chest in their own way; however, third, one refuses to register shock or disgust at whatever they say (or, put differently, one sets aside the normal course of engaging in verbal and relational reciprocity); and, finally, one manipulates the ultimate rewards in an attempt to conduce appropriate behavior, emotions, and sense of inner understanding. It is thus like a therapist who is present and allows the person full license to speak, does not show normal reactions to shocking statements, but then expects the person to see things the analyst's way as the price of support and reinclusion. The particular form this process takes is, of course, distinctive to the

Kpelle, but it is interesting to ask whether its effectiveness depends on a general style of psychological coercion and how such a process might translate into other cultures.

To a certain extent these ideas have received some testing in the procedures of the Jewish Conciliation Board of New York City. Begun in 1920, the board built on the tradition of Jewish religious courts but developed along far more secular lines. Intended to assist those who might be attracted to solving their problems through conciliation rather than lengthy and expensive litigation, and in a style that was attentive to their background and values, the board handled over a thousand cases a year by the 1960s. Most cases were, in fact, dealt with by the board's administrator, who would counsel a settlement; only a small fraction went on to a hearing. The members of the board reflected both the origins and the thrust of the institution: It included a rabbi, a lawyer, and a businessman—the latter for what the community thought represented commonsense, "unlegalistic," "real world" experience. Hearings were very informal and highly sensitive to individual personalities and circumstances. Parties agreed in advance that the solution would be written up in accordance with the provisions of the American Arbitration Association's form agreement, an agreement that could, if needed, receive enforcement in a state court. The board made effective use of flattery, apology, and no small amount of emotion: The volunteer members assumed that no two cases were truly the same inasmuch as no two people or situations were quite identical, and that each case needed individual attention.

For the first forty years or so of its existence most clients came from immigrants living on the city's Lower East Side, where the board was located. As that generation moved or died out, the board got a second breath with Russian Jewish immigrants, who, though not religious enough to go to a rabbinical court, felt comfortable with the board's style. The operation was moved to midtown Manhattan, housed with Jewish Social Services, and became increasingly integrated with a broader range of social services. In the past the board might call on a psychiatrist to sit with the panel, but by the 1980s the group was expanded to include such a professional regularly—itself, perhaps, a sign of the American tendency to regard professional assistance as a key to any kind of problem. But by the end of the century, with even the newer immigrants more dispersed and acclimatized to the country, the board was dissolved and most of its operations were melded into community social services. Like state-mandated conciliation, the experience of the board raises the question whether the effectiveness of such a format depends on the relative homogeneity of the community served and whether such a mechanism would work if it were implanted, for example, in a given neighborhood or workplace.

Tailor-made justice, like tailor-made suits, will be practical only if the tailor can devote a lot of time and personal attention to the customer. The judge's decision will be worthless unless he knows, in much more than a cursory way, the man he is judging. And not only the man but the world he comes from, the values his society lives by, the nuances of the words he uses. Such knowledge is possible only in a community court, where the judge and the judged have a mutual trust and an understanding based on a kind of family feeling.
—James Yaffe, *So Sue Me*, 1972

The standards of the law are the standards of general application. The law takes no account of the infinite varieties of temperament, intellect, and education which make the internal character of a given act so different in different men. It does not attempt to see men as God sees them.
—Oliver W. Holmes, *The Common Law*, 1881

If the Kpelle represent a psychological and the Jewish Conciliation Board a mediational model for attending to disputes, the nonpolitical trials of the former Soviet Union, as described by George Feifer, may have represented an educational model. Petty thievery from a communal enterprise or minor criminal misconduct resulted in trials, sometimes conducted at the workplace or residential compound, in which the accused was not only expected to recognize the repercussions of his antisocial behavior but to display some educability if the punishment was to be effective. Like most civil law systems, which require a trial even if there is a guilty plea, the Soviet system could be said to have as its aim the reintegration of the individual into the system, and to have marshaled everything from public shame to public confession toward that goal.

Law and the Romance of Community

At one level it seems, in many instances, as if there is a significant discrepancy between what a legal system claims to be doing and the role it actually occupies, whether from the point of view of litigants or from that of scholars analyzing legal systems for their relation to the structure of the community. We have already seen how some studies suggest that law is sometimes less about solving problems than about negotiating the normative order. Studies of smaller American communities, for example, have demonstrated two interesting propositions: first, that the interaction between the court personnel, on the one hand, and those who encounter them as victims, witnesses, or litigants, on the other, simultaneously separates the court from the rest of society and reinforces its orientations by dramati-

Fig. 3. Legal clinic in Los Angeles, 1974. (Photo by Jim Collison/TimePix.)

Fig. 4. Oklahoma land rush "law office," late nineteenth century. (University of Oklahoma Library, Norman.)

cally representing the law to all concerned. Like American culture generally, the predominant discourse of the legal system is one of individual rights, yet the image of a "good Christian" or a "proper member of one's community" or being an insider rather than a member of a minority group implies that one should not threaten community peace or demonstrate dubious ethical development by taking a case to court. Power in such communities is not primarily seen as the capacity to invoke an institution to one's benefit but as the ability to avoid being categorized as one who is so uncertain in his own eyes and those of his neighbors about the position of his group as to need his place to be defined by litigation. Thus the extent to which people feel that a court is compatible with their sense of having their concerns attended or is alienating either in its procedures or because one's self-image as a particular type of person—religious, moral, high class—is antithetical to the way one sees the law is absolutely crucial to its ability to join cultural domains or mark their boundaries.

The American romance of community is often an ideology lacking in substantial content, but the idea of "community" may have a profound effect on whether one accepts or walks away from disputes and the institutions devoted to their resolution. The ambivalence about "community" may be one of the reasons why American courts will not allow juries to be told that they may serve as the "conscience of the community":

As one court put it, such appeals "carry the potential of substantial injustice when invoked against outsiders." Thus notwithstanding the image of Americans as highly litigious—which, in both historical and comparative terms, they have actually been shown *not* to be— the meaning of legal entanglement may run counter to broader cultural values.

When Americans do go to court over interpersonal matters, however, studies show that what they commonly seek is not so much the opportunity to win their claim as to have others attend to their story. The phrase "getting one's day in court" captures this need perfectly. In the course of hearings about amending one state's family law code, for example, lawyers complained that middle-class clients simply did not get the point of no-fault divorce: They wanted the court and the lawyer to hear about the dreadful conduct of their spouses. Poorer people, by comparison, had no expectation that these personnel would be able to respond to their sense of injury, even though they preferred some form of hearing to none at all. A judge may see a particular legal process as efficient, whereas a litigant may see it as cutting off his chance to be heard. Indeed, the hidden agenda of a litigant may have mainly to do with a procedural concern—ranging from the court (rather like the Tiruray figure) validating the reason why the litigant has every "right" to be upset, to antipathy to the court's attempt to mediate differences when what litigants really want is an acceptable way to have nothing to do with one another again. As in the numerous television programs showing real cases heard by lower-level magistrates, where one sees that it is not mainly the result but the process people seek, or in the formal studies of scholars, which confirm that procedural justice may outstrip the desire for victory alone, courts that fail to respond to actual litigant needs and designs may become deeply alienated from the cultures they ostensibly serve.

Anthropologists have thus been able to show that social relationships, and the ideas that give them form, cross the boundaries of court and courtyard, office and neighborhood, marketplace and mediation with necessary ease. However alienating some forum may be to particular persons or moments in life, the information that flows through a culture is not easily dammed up. Conciliation and mediation, whatever their specific shape, reveal the limited utility of distinguishing "formal" from "informal" mechanisms: However configured in a given society, institutions operate by the lights of the concepts and relationships upon which they can draw, whether the goal they are meant to achieve is to adjudicate rights, reaffirm societal expectations, or reorient parties to the solution of their own relations. To borrow another's form, to implement a process without concern for its context, its aims, or its overtones—or to pretend that the supporting structure for a legal rule can be applied without regard to society or history—is to risk both the failure of practice and the failure to think carefully about one's theory of law and culture.

Theories of Law and Society:
A Very Brief Intellectual History

Our discussion of custom, morals, and families of law has been cast in terms of a theory of culture that might appear to claim exclusive explanatory force. But that would be misleading. For while such a theory reveals much about legal systems, theories are like different lenses, each of which may be particularly capable of revealing certain features. Depending on what it is one is trying to explain, an eclectic approach to the use of theory may be the course of wisdom.

Such is not, however, always the case among scholars and ideologues. It is one of the common features of legal and social theory to make universal claims, but in order to understand why thinking about law as culture does not mean that it is an approach that stands in contradistinction to all other approaches—or denudes them of any of their own specificity by some process of displacement or amalgamation—it may be desirable at this point to consider, however briefly, the relation of a cultural approach to others that are common to the study of legal and social systems.

Some theories appear so true for certain areas of life that one imagines they must be true for all other domains as well. If you believe that God is present in everyday life, how can you limit him to only particular areas of involvement? If you think that the laws of genetics account for the fundamental nature of any plant or animal, how can you ignore those laws when questions arise about behavior? Theories that claim total explanatory power—Marxist, structuralist, religious, and so on—possess special appeal, at least to Westerners, precisely because they seem to contain all inconsistencies and thus accord with our received sense that a unified theory of the universe must carry special persuasiveness.

Among those theories that have held persistent allure is evolutionism. After all, if evolution applies in the realm of the biological, and if an essential feature of the human animal is its capacity for social organization and conceptual elaboration, then how could evolution not apply to various institutions, including law? Indeed, who can look at legal systems and not see evolution at work: Have "we" not, as any sensible person can see, "progressed" from private revenge to collective rules, from the "irrational" use of oath or ordeal to the refinements of forensic science? Indeed, much of the "proof" that societies and their legal systems must be subject to some version of the forces of evolution can be said to reside precisely in the fact that evolutionary theory does not point in some inevitable direction or imply any value-laden claim to ultimate purpose: It is simply a coherent theory that unites many phenomena under a single analytic frame.

Such ideas of evolution have been applied to law in a variety of ways. Sir Henry Maine, quite famously, spoke of the transition from status to contract in human societies—the development of interpersonal agreements in place of restrictive attachments based on birth or position. Maine was operating in an environment of social Darwinism, when so many aspects of human society were thought to be informed by— and, as a matter of policy, should be directed in concert with—the dictates of adaptation, variation, and indeed survival of the fittest as set forth in the realm of biology. In studies of society this orientation contributed to the quest for origins—whether in Tyler's account of religion, Spencer's of social forms, or Engels's of political types—just as one could seek the origin of the species. Evolutionism played its role, too, in actual legal decision-making: Oliver Wendell Holmes clearly thought that the state should not get in the way of social evolutionary forces working themselves through to the preferable ideas, whether in the marketplace or the political forum. And Karl Marx, like his occasional collaborator Friedrich Engels, assumed that the progression from capitalism through socialism to communism had natural, and not simply ideological, properties. By the mid–twentieth century, when there was a renewal of cultural evolutionary thought in anthropology, many of the scholars associated with the department at the University of Michigan (Leslie White, Marshall Sahlins, and a number of archaeologists) set forth actual laws that were based on such notions as the greater capture of energy by one society over another or "the law of evolutionary potential" that allows a "backward" society to leap over a stage of development at which others may be stuck in order to move directly to a more advanced level. In his *Germs, Guns and Steel,* Jared Diamond still relies on the Michigan approach, long after many of its proponents rejected it, for his geographically deterministic view of a "science of human history."

The problems with all of these approaches to cultural evolution—whether applied to law or any other domain—have come in several varieties. First, no one has persuasively specified the precise mechanisms through which social evolution is purported to operate. What is the cultural or social equivalent of genetic drift, mutation, or genetic flow; what, indeed, is the operative unit comparable to the gene? Some have argued that population increase or institutional elaboration is the sociocultural equivalent of these biological mechanisms: The Michigan anthropologists, for example, characterized cultural evolution as determinable by structural complexity and functional specificity. But these features are hardly on the same level as those discerned by modern biology. Indeed, the very idea that one social form is more evolved than another, even though it implies no greater claim to superiority of one form over another than a claim that dogs are more evolved than ants, has proved inadequate even in its most "apparent" instance, the development of political forms. The classic evolutionary formulation of band, tribe, chieftain, and state became the governing paradigm. But this arrangement, convenient for archaeologists and alluring for those who had begun to look beyond classic anthropological subjects ("primitive" societies) to emergent nations and other "complex" societies, did not fit the facts. Tribes may actually come into existence only in the presence of states; large African kingdoms possess some of the features of states but not others; multiple forms might coexist within a single culture. The idea of evolution as anything more than a metaphor for development, change, growth, or (in a fashion that appeals to Western ideas of history) "progress" could never get beyond the level of mere analogy to the mechanisms that would have to be specified were evolution, in any precise sense, to be the applicable explanation of social and cultural change. As Stephen Jay Gould, who described himself as "especially wary of 'soft' and overly pat analogies between biological evolution and human cultural change," has said, the idea of a "great chain of being" is not an ineluctable mode of organization but "an indefensible conceit."

While the absolute types and patterns proposed by earlier evolutionists are no longer accepted by legal anthropologists in view of the diversity of social patterns in human history, the basic evolutionary principle assuming a correlation between

(box continues on next page)

(continued)

the legal and social order of given societies has become a commonplace in social thought. . . . Logic as well as anthropological observation suggest that legal development is related to the growth of social organization. . . . In general, the sophistication of the legal system corresponds to the size and density of the population. . . . The evidence is overwhelmingly persuasive that societies at the same level in their evolution, regardless of their chronological position in history, develop laws that display remarkable similarities.

—Theodore Ziolkowski, *The Mirror of Justice*

Biological evolution is a bad analogue for cultural change because the two systems are so different for three major reasons that could hardly be more fundamental. First, cultural evolution can be faster by orders of magnitude than biological change at its maximum Darwinian rate—and questions of timing are of the essence in evolutionary arguments. Second, cultural evolution is direct and Lamarckian in form: The achievements of one generation are passed by education and publication directly to the descendants, thus

(box continues on next page)

> *(continued)*
>
> producing the great potential speed of cultural change. . . . Third, the basic typologies of biological and cultural change are completely different. Biological evolution is a system of constant divergence without subsequent joining of branches. Lineages, once distinct, are separate forever. In human history, transmission across lineages is, perhaps, the major source of cultural change.
> —Stephen Jay Gould, *Bully for Brontosaurus*

And yet the image retains its attraction. Not only do most anthropology textbooks continue to use the scheme of stages of political development when the rest of the book consistently undermines it, but legal scholars continue to write in this idiom as well. Theodore Ziolkowski's argument in *The Mirror of Justice* that European law evolves from earlier forms and Richard Schwartz's claim that a distinct legal forum develops in those Israeli communes where private property emerges are two such examples. Once again, the seemingly commonsense notion that legal systems have gotten more complex seems to attract the word *evolution* without ever attracting a basis for explanation comparable to that found in the biological sciences.

In Great Britain, a sharp reaction to social evolution developed in the years surrounding the Second World

War. Fearful of being drawn by evolutionism into issues
of origins about which no proofs could ever be forthcoming, and perhaps in reaction to the Whig view of
history—that all was headed in the direction of British
society as it had come to exist—anthropologists moved
in quite a different direction. Under the sometime
changing rubrics of functionalism and structural-func-
tionalism, they set out to determine the precise forms
of social organization that characterize a given society
and the ways in which various institutions contribute
to the operation of the whole. While the metaphors of
what a society was like varied—an organism, a mechanical device, or (to later scholars, often operating under
the influence of Lévi-Straussian structuralism) a language—they did demonstrate that societies are orderly. That may seem a trivial point, but it is actually
one of the most stunning demonstrations of modern
scholarship. Previously, "primitive" thought was regarded as childlike, mistaken, or irrational; social
forms of "simple" societies were imagined as either literally simple or incoherent. What these scholars
showed, however, was that every society is highly organized, that it possesses a logic that is recoverable by
careful analysis. More than that, they demonstrated
that these previously misunderstood societies possess
religious ideas that (to borrow Evans-Pritchard's characterization of the Nuer) are deserving of the term *the-
ology* or (to borrow Max Gluckman's characterization
of the legal system of the Barotse) constitute a system

of jurisprudence. In a very real sense, to use yet another metaphor that has become common in many
fields of social science, these scholars really did crack
the code of societies: They demonstrated that all societies are organized, however variously, in ways that are
highly sophisticated and that only a full-scale analysis
of how all of their social, political, legal, and religious
institutions connect to one another can reveal their
particular form of organization for what it is.

The specific contributions in what came to be denominated *legal anthropology* were not insignificant
parts of this development. Not only was the term *law*
now made applicable to even nonliterate societies, but
the precise range of ways they settled disputes became
a point of entry to their broader political and economic structure. But despite the contribution of important ethnographic examples, the structural-func-
tionalist approach had several general limitations, one
of which has proved particularly limiting for those who
have pursued legal analysis in its terms. For while functionalism revealed connections one might not have
thought about—that trade networks mapped kinship
connections, or that witchcraft accusations revealed
points of tension in social relations—it is a theory that
cannot explain change. If societies are, like a thermo-
stat, self-righting mechanisms—so that, for example,
when someone is accidentally injured, a witchcraft
accusation works not like punishment but like a social insurance scheme, or that feuds place limi-

tations on violence so that disputes do not develop into
the war of all against all—then how can one ever account for alterations in the system as a whole? And if
society is like an organism—kinship as the heart, religion as the head, politics as the limbs—are we simply
to assume that growth, florescence, and decay are the
mechanisms that account for alteration? The inability
to account for history—avoided by the British for fear
of regressing to claims of evolution and origins, unin-
viting to many American anthropologists who were
fearful of the loss of disciplinary identity—yielded
some unfortunate results: Evans-Pritchard did not real-
ize he was seeing Nuer society at a particular moment
in its political history, not some perduring structure;
Malinowski did not appreciate that gender and colo-
nialism were playing a vital role in what was happening
to "crime and custom" among the Trobriand Islanders.

But the structural-functionalists on both sides of the
Atlantic who were studying legal systems have made a
mistake that, while hard to pinpoint, has been almost
unique to their subdiscipline: They have contributed
almost nothing to the development of anthropological
theory. This is apparent in numerous ways. Anthropologists who are not interested in law almost never read
even the most well known monographs of those studying law. Excellent works—like Lloyd Fallers's *Law Without Precedent* or Stuart Schlegel's *Tiruray Justice*—never
even made it into paperback: "Classics," like Paul Bo-
hannon's *Justice and Judgment among the Tiv* or Max

Gluckman's *Barotse Jurisprudence,* are (as one says of many classics) more often mentioned than read. There are various reasons that may account for this lack of contribution to the discipline as a whole. For one, many American scholars have undeniable prejudice against law. Like their countrymen, they tend to think of law as a domain of specialists, rife with strange terminology and far from disinterested maneuvering. The claim is then made, often in a tone of solidarity with those ostensibly oppressed or alienated by the law, that it is only in the extralegal, "informal" domain that the real law of the people takes place. So courts are shunned as field sites, and "informal" dispute settlement mechanisms are emphasized. The result, however, is that the focus still remains narrowly tied to the idea of disputing, and even within this circumscribed definition—where one may discuss the multiple levels available or the crafty ways that state intrusiveness may be averted—there is no focus on law as a domain in which a wide range of ideas and relationships that are central to studies of religion or kinship or economic structures may be at work. The result is that other scholars, either put off by the mistaken idea that law is any more "uncharacteristic" of a society or any more unavailable than the church, the marketplace, or the men's house, can find confirmation for their orientation by simply avoiding the field. When this is joined with the tendency of most students of law and society to be either structural-functionalists in their implicit theoretical approach or to be intensely particularistic in their studies, the discipline at large has little difficulty ignoring their potential contributions to theory at large.

Natural law has been another prominent approach to legal systems, and it has made a comeback in recent years. Like evolutionism, it is almost irresistible to think that there are principles that must transcend time and place—that support for relationships like marriage allow each individual to flourish, that people do indeed possess inner states to which proper attention must be paid, or that the punishment can always be found that fits the crime. Such approaches arise almost entirely from particular religious traditions, so that the natural law of Christians, Muslims, or Native Americans share the claim to cosmic truth despite the enormous differences they may display in content. Some Catholic legal scholars and judges, in particular, have elaborated and employed natural law in their writings and judgments in recent years: The reference by Justice Scalia to "evidence*s*" (i.e., signs of God's truth) in the creationism decision or to "our long tradition of *contra bonos mores*" are founded on the natural law background of canon and civil law notions. But like evolutionism, the assertion of specific propositions of natural law reveals more about the accepted common sense of a cultural system than a demonstrable universal. The theory of culture on which the present study is based, it will be recalled, suggests that when the com-

ponents of a culture are replicated across familial, religious, economic, literary, political, and legal bounds,
they take on the appearance of being both immanent
and natural. Thus, from this perspective there is no
such thing as natural law, there is only law naturalized.
That any given system may see its law as a feature of
nature only intensifies the argument that legal systems
always seem to require some claim to authority outside
of their own creative domain as part of their broader
claim to legitimacy.

In recent years one also finds a much more overtly
political approach to the study of law. This largely skeptical view, sometimes associated with "critical studies"
of one emphasis or another, developed at the same
time in law that deconstruction was developing in literary studies. Like that orientation, it seeks to take apart
the presumed structure of a legal system and reveal its
attachments to power and its manipulations of knowledge. So, for example, the economic interests of the
legal establishment will be cited for the development
of a doctrine of tort liability, or the ways in which race
or gender have been constructed in society at large will
be found to be inseparable from the rules of evidence
or the presumptions at work in police stations or court-
houses. These studies have often been of enormous
value. We now have a much better understanding of
how it is, say, that women get charged higher prices for
automobiles than do men or how jurors evaluate black
defendants differently from whites. At the same time,

like legal anthropology, the contributions to theory
have been all but absent. Whereas, for a generation,
gender studies in anthropology and history, for example, have done far more for our understanding of the
structure and operation of society than any other
branch of study, critical legal studies, for all its demon-
stration of biases present in a system, has not led to
new ideas about the relations among law, society, and
culture in any more generalized sense. Like the law-
and-economics movement, which has captivated
American legal education, but which has also been
largely devoid of contribution to economic theory, the
reasons for this failure may lie in several places. First,
at a time when all politics has gone from being local
to being personal, critical studies allows the investiga-
tor to claim solidarity with (indeed, in anthropology,
to be the voice, and in law the advocate, for) the under-
dog, and thus one can combine personal commitment
with scholarly task. That this may, in many instances,
be personally praiseworthy does not alter the fact that
under its banner one can criticize predecessors for
their political naïveté or bias while forgiving oneself of
any such charge. More pointedly, the scholarly disad-
vantage of this stance lies in the fact that one must
begin and end with law as one's subject, even though
many of the issues these scholars take up should lead
them into domains other than law itself. Yet because
they are residents of law faculties or law courts, the
sociology of their knowledge rechannels all of their
efforts back into the domain of formal law. If, again,

approaching law as culture has merit precisely because culture is the stitching together across domains of the categories of experience and the relationships that are connected to them, then failing to follow issues (intent, fact-determination, ideas of human nature and relationship, etc.) across these analytic lines must necessarily limit contributions to cultural and legal theory.

It has been said that even in the law the penalties for trespass are very light. Yet the structure of knowledge within the academy and the legal systems of Western countries is such that crossing boundaries is often strongly discouraged. If fishmongers think there is nothing so marvelous as fish and cattlemen think there is nothing so wonderful as beef, students of law think there is nothing so central to knowledge as understanding the law—even if the result is to say that it is not all it is cracked up to be. But if there is solid reason to regard law as part of culture, and if ideas about their relationship are to transcend butterfly collecting or resist all-embracing assertions, then we have to return to the basic claim of this study—to see, through comparative instances, how parts of a society and culture may be connected to one another and then to bring these possibilities, both as generalizations and as heuristic devices, back to a fuller understanding of the particulars of a given system. It is to just such an endeavor that thinking about the creation of facts invites us.

CHAPTER 2

Creating Facts

> In the study of ideas, it is necessary
> to remember that insistence on
> hardheaded clarity issues from
> sentimental feeling, as it were a
> mist, cloaking the perplexities of
> fact. Insistence on clarity at all costs
> is based on sheer superstition as
> to the mode in which human intelli-
> gence functions. Our reasonings
> grasp at straws for premises and
> float on gossamers for deductions.
> —Alfred North Whitehead,
> *Adventures in Ideas*

Legal "Facts" and Cultural History:
Britain and the Continent

Legal systems create facts in order to treat them as
facts. Even when there is little dispute over what "really" happened, something must first be regarded as a

fact if it is to count as such. If, for example, you believe that there are clear indicators of an individual's religious beliefs or personal intent, or that someone's poverty, gender, or education is crucial to an understanding of his or her acts; if you think you can determine honesty by demeanor or that a series of moral gradations actually tracks reality, then assertions will hold truth-value for you that, for those living in other times and places, they simply do not. In addition, a legal system may set the boundaries of a case narrowly or very widely. If, say, the issue that precipitated the action was a divorce, but the mediator or trier of fact sees it as really a dispute over property between the spouses' kin, he may, depending on the system's goals, open the matter up to broader concerns. In other systems, like the courts of most Western countries, there is a kind of "skeletalizing" of the facts, as the issue is narrowed to one the decision-maker is thought capable and authorized to make. Thus, to choose an American example, a person accused of a crime may bring witnesses to his character, but they may not discuss specific actions in which he engaged, only his general reputation in the community: Oddly, perhaps, only rumor, not actual events, may be offered in evidence. Faced, as H.L.A. Hart put it, with the twinned problem of "our relative ignorance of fact" and "our relative indeterminacy of aim," each legal system must address its goals and its construction of the believable simultaneously. Whether skeletalized or fleshed out, a society's legal process will, then, be characterized by its way of creating categories of the knowable and relating them to the ways in which facts are constructed in the culture at large.

No story better demonstrates the link between cultural and legal "facts," as well as the ways they have changed in relation to one another over the course of time, than does the history of the development of the British jury as contrasted with the development of fact-finding on the European continent. In retelling this story, however briefly, one has to tack between institutional and cultural history to see how changes the law brings to society are balanced with changes that occur in such diverse realms as religion, literature, and the emerging concept of the person. As judges and juries replace private actions and the invocation of divine justice, a changing set of assumptions about law, society, and human nature reveal themselves with striking force.

The Development of the Jury

At the time of the Norman invasions the conquerors set a pattern that has reverberated through British history up to and including the high-water mark of the empire. Few in number and hardly welcomed by the Anglo-Saxon population, the Normans applied a political system that much later came to be referred to as "indirect rule." This approach had two main effects: the use of local institutions as the basis for the conquerors'

minority rule, and the use of law as a preeminent vehicle for the centralization of the state—mechanisms that
remained applicable to the rule of India and other British colonies no less than for the Norman invaders.

A key form that Norman indirect rule took involved
holding people co-liable for misdeeds committed
within the territories of their local groupings unless,
upon discovery of the crime, they raised the "hue and
cry" so as to distance themselves from any act committed by stealth. By compelling everyone but clerics,
knights, and lords to enroll in groups that would be
held collectively responsible if they failed to present
an accused, the Normans could, particularly when the
monarchy was relatively weak, use the locals to do
much of their policing for them. Royal judges helped
frame the questions but, through the use of local fact-
finding institutions, largely left it to the locals to
decide specific cases. As H. Patrick Glenn remarks:
"Local people couldn't object much to royal justice if
they themselves controlled the decisions, and reliance
on local ways gave needed legitimacy to the royal process." Though appeals were costly, they could be taken
to the king, and royal jurisdiction was gradually increased at the expense of manorial courts, the barons
actually acquiescing in the extension of the "King's
Peace" since the property of those found guilty were
turned over to them.

Fact-finding itself, at least for the first century after
the Conquest, is said to have consisted primarily of the

use of "irrational" methods, particularly ordeals and oaths. In the absence of witnesses the people of late antiquity and the early Middle Ages called upon divine judgment with some regularity. But to characterize the oaths and ordeals as simply "irrational" modes of proof can be misleading. Even if the term is meant to denote modes of proof that are not subject to human inspection, there was still a good deal of human involvement before matters might be turned over to the divine. Not only were facts seldom in contention—as people were deeply involved in face-to-face relations, and privacy was all but unknown—but the assessment was less of a deed than of a person. The question was "who is most likely to have committed the act," an appraisal based mainly on that person's status, past actions, and overall reputation. Without at this point reifying the concept of probability, the presentment of the accused can be said to have followed on a kind of probable cause assessment, itself far from an "irrational" mode of thought. Moreover, as comparative examples suggest, fact and law were undoubtedly conjoined by knowledge of local circumstance: Jural principles were linked to an interpretation of acts and persons, and the "irrational" modes of proof were meant to bring law and fact together, rather than (as in later forms of procedure) to encourage acting as if one could not tell them apart.

"Irrational" proofs (called "wagers of law") took various forms. The Anglo-Saxons relied a good deal on

collective oath-taking, or compurgation. If the appropriate number of co-swearers, usually close kinsmen,
were presented and swore in accordance with the rigorously required wording, the defendant would pre-
vail. With central authority weak, concern to avoid
feuding increasing, and compurgation a vehicle for
the public ascertainment of allies' loyalties, it served
not to determine what happened but, in a larger sense,
to preclude too much from happening. As in those
more recent instances where compurgation has been
studied (in Africa, say, or among the Berbers), the use
of co-swearers may have limited violence and introduced a pause in actions that might otherwise draw
reluctant associates into unsought disputes. To this day
in Crete, as Michael Herzfeld has argued, oath-taking
is mainly a vehicle for interrupting the cycle of suspicion that accompanies demonstrations of manliness
through sheep stealing: The oath, taken at just those
times when matters may adversely affect a wide network of others, "momentarily appears to reconstitute
the fractured perfection of reciprocity." In the Anglo-
Saxon case, whether by means of oath or ordeal, the
decision of the court before which the accusation was
made was not of the merits but of the mode by which
a person would then be put to his or her "proof."

It was the Normans who introduced trial by battle
as the favored form of the ordeal. Initiated by a single
accuser (though now in strict written form) and
hedged round with religious ritual, the loser in a crimi-

Fig. 5. Engraving of knights engaged in trial by battle,
fifteenth century woodcut. (Library of Congress.)

nal case, if not slain in the contest, usually did not survive long, as he was commonly executed following his
defeat. Stables of champions were kept by those, including the church, who were frequently involved in
civil suits. It may not, however, only have been the skepticism that accompanied recognition that God seemed
to favor the strong that eventually undermined trial by
battle. Henry II (1154–1189) distrusted the older
modes of proof, saw in the presentment by locals a vehicle for bringing private disputes under public control,
and had even begun to use a panel of twelve to decide
property disputes between laymen and clergy. The
monarchy thus sought to extend its control through
indirect rule and to regularize these new procedures,
on the hundredth anniversary of the Conquest and fol-

lowing more than a decade of civil war, through the reforms undertaken by the ordinance Henry promulgated, known as the Assize of Clarendon.

The Normans had already set a pattern for the common law by their emphasis on procedure (more than substantive rules) and, as we shall see, by narrowing the issues that could get to local decision-makers through the issuance of a permit (or writ) that allowed a given issue, claim, or defense in a legal proceeding. The Assize of Clarendon basically organized the presentment of those accused of serious crimes, in what was now clearly a royal event, by requiring a group of twelve accusers to make their charge under oath, after which an individual ordeal, now largely replacing battle, would go forward. The sheriff was required to take all presentments, which then went before a regular circuit court or an itinerant royal justice at an infrequent sort of legal and taxing fair, called an eyre. These judges began to apply the same laws wherever they went, a common law, and thus helped not only to assert the role of laymen, as opposed to clerics, in the management of legal affairs but to create a law that was so widely shared that arrangements predating Henry's time came to be regarded as prior to the formation of the common law of the realm.

The ordeal itself might involve various methods, from holding a hot iron to being submerged in a stream or pond. Discretion was certainly in play, as the decision whether someone's hand was really healed or whether he had indeed bobbed to the surface (as, unnaturally,

In nomni loco dnationis ei. benedicam
ma mea dno. D s madiutonu meu
untende. Dne ad adiuuandu me festh

Fig. 6. Ordeal of cold water. (From the facsimile in *Monumenta Germaniae Historiae*," reprinted in John Henry Wigmore, *A Panorama of World Legal Systems*, vol. 2 [St. Paul: West, 1928], 859.)

only a guilty person aided by the devil would do) might involve some interpretation. Interestingly, even if a person passed the ordeal but was regarded as having a bad reputation, the accused was required to "abjure the realm," that is, to leave the country by set route and time or be subject to death at anyone's hand. Clearly, then, the "facts" were still largely assessments of persons, who might, in theory, be banished for ill-repute even though not found wanting in the ordeal. Clearly, too, we see the precursor to the trial jury (and, more directly, to the later grand jury) in the jury of presentment, which comes (as does its successor for several more centuries) "to speak more than to hear." Indeed, as a means of indirect rule, the system regularized by the Assize of Clarendon was a notable achievement: It usually drew on local people and their local culture, it required few public officials and dispersed the potential for corruption, it increased centralized authority, and it was consistent with then existing concepts of divine intervention and the nature of human nature.

A large cask had been set up and filled with water. The young man who was the object of suspicion was pinioned, suspended from a rope by his shoulder-blades, and plunged into the cask. If he was innocent, they said, he would sink into the water, and they would pull him out by the rope. If he was guilty, it would be impossible for him to sink into the water. When he was thrown into the cask, the unfortunate man made every effort to descend to the bottom, but he could not manage it, and thus had to submit to the rigors of their law—may God's curse be upon them! He was then blinded by a red-hot silver awl.
—Usamah Ibn Munqidh (1095–1188), a Muslim witness to such ordeals among the Crusaders in Syria

The Law on the Continent

The story on the Continent centers more on the role of the church and the rediscovery of late Roman law.

Both canon law procedures and civil administration
had been much affected by the study of such classical
sources of law as the Code of Justinian, studies that
were predominantly initiated at the secular University
of Bologna. From merely retranscribing the texts to
writing glosses on them, students were developing fa-
miliarity with written sources and the habits of organizing and arranging legal materials. Thus, while many of
the same accusatorial processes found in Britain pre-
vailed on the Continent through to the early thirteenth century, the seeds of divergence had been
planted, and it only took the actions of Pope Innocent
III to set them firmly on their separate courses.

The year 1215 is, of course, best known in the Anglo-
phonic world for Magna Carta, and, quite aside from
its well-known effects on the distribution of powers between king and barons, that document was not without
its legal import. It guaranteed several procedures that
had entered practice over the years, from regular circuit hearings to verdict by locals in civil cases when both
parties agreed to it. In addition, it eliminated the cost
involved in seeking a royal writ claiming that one had
been accused out of "spite and malice," a writ that
would allow a group of decision-makers to hear a claim
of biased accusation. It even responded to the barons'
desire for more frequent sessions held in the counties
by royal judges, though even the one per year promised
when the charter was reissued in 1217 appears to have
been beyond the organizational capacities of the cen-

Fig. 7. Glossed civil code. (From John Henry Wigmore, *A Panorama of World Legal Systems*, vol. 3 [St. Paul: West, 1928].)

tral government. In these and other instances, though still embedded in a system of ordeals, the precursors of modern institutions are, then, clearly discernible.

The act that precipitated continentals and British alike to reflect on their legal proceedings, however, was the other great event of 1215, the Fourth Lateran

Council. Under Pope Innocent's leadership, the church removed the priests from participation in the administration of the ordeals, and with God out of the picture something had to be found by way of replacement. In Britain that became the jury as the finder of fact; on the Continent it became the inquiring judge trained in the methods of the church and supported by the clerks who had attended institutions where Roman law was being rediscovered.

Although a number of scholars have argued that the ordeals declined as soon as clerical opposition received papal confirmation, the stronger argument, by no less distinguished analysts, holds that the change did not happen overnight any more than loss of confidence in the ordeals had. Nor was the groundwork for the abolition of the ordeals a narrowly clerical, scholarly, or political matter. Churchmen had, it is true, attacked the ordeals as an un-Christian attempt to force God to act on human command and, quite aside from the absence of their mention in the Bible, stories abounded in literature and common parlance of guilty parties who nevertheless passed an ordeal. But the twelfth century was a period of broad-scale cultural change. It not only marked the rise of the cities and the concomitant diminution in some ties of kinship and locale, but it also marked major changes in the ideas about people themselves. In literature, we see the shift from the epic to the romance, and with it the emphasis on the individual's thoughts and reasons. Men like Bernard of Clairvaux and Chrétien de Troyes declared that people have an interior existence, and that God will see into these inner selves, and not just to overt acts and utterances, in judging them. A language of intent accompanied religious change as Christ, so long represented as dead upon the cross, became a living, suffering figure, and the Virgin Mary became a focus of entreaty as she looked to the supplicant's feelings and emotions. In law, strict liability offenses began to give way, and the idea of individual intent began to inform a wide range of offenses. Certainly confidence in the old forms of proof had been diminished by their corruption and the criticism of intellectuals, but far greater conceptual trends were in play when Lateran effectively ended the ordeals.

> [The ordeal] is not in accord with nature and does not lead to truth. . . . How could a man believe that the natural heat of glowing iron will become cool or cold without an adequate cause . . . or that because of a seared conscience the element of cold water will refuse to accept the accused? . . . These judgments of God by ordeal which men call "truth-revealing" might better be called "truth-concealing."
> —Frederick II, Holy Roman Emperor and king of Sicily (1194–1250)

But what to do? After all, if God judged through the ordeals and he was never wrong, if men were to presume to replace such a judge and such a standard of

Fig. 8. In the tenth century, the wife of Emperor Otto III, forced to hold the head of her alleged lover in one hand and a hot iron in the other, fails the ordeal and is seen in the background being burned at the stake. (Oil on panel by Dierik (Dirk) Bouts, *Justice of Emperor Otto III*, right panel, 1470–75; Musée Royaux Des Beaux-Arts, Brussels.)

proof, what devices could possibly claim comparable legitimacy? The answer, tentative and needing much development, came differently on each side of the Channel.

The government in Britain initially told its judges: "We leave it to your discretion; proceed according to your good sense and conscience, ascertaining as far as you can the character of the individuals involved, the nature of the crime and the truth of the matter." But in short order the British began to turn to several ways in which cases could be decided by others from the community. Consensual trial ("putting oneself on one's country") did exist as an alternative to the ordeal, consent being necessary if men were to substitute as judges for God. Similarly, the writ against spiteful accusations sent cases back for human decision, as did challenges alleging some or all of the jurors to be interested parties. But to transform the jury of presentment into a trial jury took time. At first, "consent" was sought through coercion—starvation or placing weights on the defendant's chest (*peine forte et dure*). Initially, too, as the presenting jury became an indicting jury (not all of whose members were likely to bring personal knowledge of the facts to the decision), as many as two dozen knights had to be impaneled to overcome the unease about human judgment. Unanimity of the jury gave something of the appearance of oracular decision-making, as well as a measure of protection to both jurors and judges. (Indeed, it was thought so im-

portant that if jurors did not reach a unanimous verdict they might be locked up or carted around the
countryside with the circuit-riding judge until they did
reach a verdict.) Cheap to operate and consistent with
the politics of indirect rule, the jury was gradually
transformed into a body that found facts (usually by
personal knowledge but sometimes through inquiry)
and that applied—indeed, even determined—the law.
In that transformation, the emergent jury encapsu-
lated and prompted many of the conceptual alterations of its day.

[A]fter the inquest was sworn they [the jurors]
could not agree.
[Judge] Stanton: Good people, you cannot
agree?
[To John Allen, Keeper of the Rolls:] Go and put
them in a house until Monday, and let them not
eat or drink.
On that commandment John put them in a house
without [food or drink].
At length on the same day about vesper-time they
agreed.
—Yearbook 3 and 4, Edward II (1310),
   Selden Society

If the Britons could turn to the incipient jury, the
Europeans could turn to the twinned devices of an in-

Fig. 9. *Jury Dead Lock,* Daniel Celantano, 1930s. (Courtesy Janet Marqusee Fine Arts, New York.)

quiring judge and the culture of the clerks. A single judge, assisted by professional staff, and himself trained in the art of discerning "truth," became the substitute for the discredited ordeals. These secular judges were not unlike ecclesiastical judges who, in a bishop's court, made similar inquiries, and the influence of canon law and its procedures was quite im-

portant to the development of Continental law. Setting
as the standard "full," or virtually absolute, proof and
increasingly acting in concert with, rather than as a
counterbalance to, the rising monarchies, the process
took on the qualities of an incipient bureaucracy. Particularly with the onset of the heresy inquisition—
which, for the most part, was keen to ferret out only
true heretics rather than serve as a general witch
hunt—the techniques of inquiry gained regularity.
Among the most dramatic, of course, was the use of
torture.

Torture as a fact-finding mechanism did not exist in
England—except in some of the later political proceedings of one royal prerogative court, the Star Chamber.
On the Continent, however, torture was used to determine facts. Though Rome had previously condemned
the use of torture, in 1251 Pope Innocent IV (d. 1254)
approved its use by the Inquisition. In theory, there
were strict rules for the application of torture: that it
could be used only to get information in the exclusive
knowledge of the guilty, or that testimony had to be
confirmed by the accused when no longer under the
threat of torture. No doubt subject to abuse, these
methods nevertheless contributed to the development
of other legal institutions: rigorous record-keeping,
professional preparation, and—perhaps most importantly—the view of law as an arm of central authority, whether that of church or state. Thus fact-finding
was not pushed down to local residential or private

Fig. 10. Trial court in Prague, 1536. From an engraving by
C. Hennig in "Chronik von Böhmen," Prague, 1852.

practitioners as in England, nor was the determination
of local practice incorporated on the Continent
through the indirect voice of local juries. Instead it de-
pended on the writings of scholars, legislators, and the
techniques of an inquiring judge. In both instances,

however, law and culture changed together: The legal focus on the person could only make sense as the concept of the person changed in religion and representation; the authority of an inquiring judge partook of the impersonal application of codifications that mirrored yet transcended their pre-Christian sources. Legal fact-finding, as in every age, became an index of the commonsense apprehension of the world even as it was increasingly molded by the specialists it cast up.

Managing Doubt

A similar connection between law and culture appears in the West some centuries later with the introduction of the concept of probability. Law, it has been said, is in many respects "a way of managing doubt," and surely the development of British and Continental law in the years following 1215 represent just such a concern. But doubt incorporates both issues of authority and degrees of certainty, and the way each of these moved in relation to the other changed markedly in the seventeenth century. Until then, rules of evidence were virtually nonexistent in Britain. Indeed, throughout the West the very term *probable* meant "authoritative," as in the authoritative reading of sacred text. As the Protestant Reformation took hold, as science struggled with levels of certainty, and as standards for grading moral acts diversified, law—as generator and as recipient—changed accordingly.

British judges of the early modern period who sought to guide juries in the applicable standards of proof were able to turn to the ways in which things were coming to be assessed as true in numerous other domains. By the mid–sixteenth century witnesses were compelled to testify, and perjury had become a crime, but degrees of certainty had not moved much beyond the civil law's idea of "full" proof—calculated by the weight of diverse forms of evidence and still affected by the idea of approximating confessional certainty— while British case law left jurors to the mysteries of their unexplained agreement. But knowledge in science and religion was undergoing a change, one whose terms became widely shared throughout the cultures of the West. The poles of certainty and mere opinion were now divided between the certainties of one's senses and deductions, on the one hand, and, on the other, an elaboration of "moral certainties" founded on secondary information. Whether it is the case that, in the field of law, sixteenth- and seventeen-century scholars built on the work of those who had glossed the texts of ancient writers and who, in deriving from them general principles, kept alive the ancients' ideas of degrees of rational belief, or whether the elaboration of probability was an independent development of their own age, two things at least are clear: A new way of knowing truth was emerging, one that suffused the terminology of so many domains of life as to constitute a new way of seeing reality in every area it touched.

Specifically, as moral categories began to develop, general terms like "conjecture," "wavering," "distrust," and "disbelief" were replaced by the concepts of "moral certainty" and "reasonable doubt." These latter terms took on increasing specificity: Measuring them on a scale marking ever higher degrees of confidence, philosophers like John Locke, the thinkers of the Scottish Enlightenment, and increasing numbers of writers of legal treatises could point to such categories as reflecting, on the one hand, the Protestant demand that, in matters of conscience, no one should simply defer to the authority of another, and, on the other, the belief that such categories should be justified by their utility in domains beyond those in which they were generated. As Barbara Shapiro notes: "When everyday life, matters of fact, historical experience, and religious belief are treated as intermediate realms between absolute, logically demonstrable knowledge and mere opinion," men of letters, journalists, clergymen, and jurists could be "prepared to face the imperfections of all human knowledge and, nevertheless, seek that intermediate goal which they called moral certainty." In short, a new vocabulary of probability was developing, one that spanned multiple domains and, like any really powerful cultural concept, knit those domains together in a distinctly "modern" form of common sense.

What were seen as criteria for appraisal in science, religion, and philosophy were not only sources for the lawyers seeking guidance for juries but, increasingly, as self-evident categories that needed not greater precision of definition but a greater range of applicable instances. This combination of extradomainal validation and casuistic reasoning allowed the "facts" to garner appropriate levels of certitude. Some commentators proposed the actual mathematizing of each form of evidence produced: Continentals thus spoke of "half proofs" and "quarter proofs" based largely on a person's status, while Jeremy Bentham proposed a "thermometer of persuasion." Where once Aquinas could address uncertainty by seeking to bring passions and will into alignment with divinely sanctioned goals, medieval thinkers began to imagine reconciling passions with individual thought so as to align such thoughts with virtues that lead to a proper end. The innovations of early modern Europe, in turn, firmly established that what lay within the individual was not a microcosm of universal truth but a world set apart from that of others. Indeed, this world was itself in need of active engagement if it was to be brought into harmony with a person's interior state. And once the concept of probability took hold, its capacity to serve as a device for grasping the world produced dramatic consequences in all the areas of cultural knowledge it touched.

In British and American law, for example, the idea of reasonable doubt became the standard for jury determinations in criminal cases. Equated at times with the philosophers' "satisfactory evidence" and frequently described as "such a level as one would not hesitate to act upon," the idea of reasonable doubt has, to the present day, retained precisely the kind of imprecision one often associates with key cultural concepts generally. Some proponents of the death penalty in the United States have thus sought to raise the standard for conviction from "beyond a reasonable doubt" to "beyond any doubt" or "to a moral certainty." In 1994, the U.S. Supreme Court upheld capital convictions in which the charge to the jury equated reasonable doubt with confidence "to a moral certainty." Although most of the justices characterized this phrase as antiquated, possibly confusing, and no longer the mainstay of our moral lexicon, the Court nevertheless found itself unable to reject the underlying idea that jurors must rely on some general sense of moral weight as they address their own degree of doubt. The resulting position left some of the justices in a quandary.

Justice Ginsburg, for example, expressed the irony of leaving the concept of reasonable doubt so poorly defined when she cited a lower-court judge saying: "I find it rather unsettling that we are using a formulation that we believe will become less clear the more we explain it." But this may simply be a specific instance of the point that the anthropologist Max Gluckman made generally when he said that "the 'certainty' of law depends on the 'uncertainty' of its basic concepts." As in art and politics, many of the central precepts of any legal scheme are ultimately inseparable from the cultural constructs that render them meaningful. And if the elaboration and the sharing of such categories are the way our species retains the ability to change and adapt, then the maintenance of open-textured, contestable concepts may, ironically, give many legal systems precisely that degree of flexible response to the larger cultural process which often makes law an institution through which we monitor our own creations.

The legal creation of facts thus summarizes and stimulates our sense of reality. That we place greater reliance on the "facts" adduced by official investigation than on statements volunteered by witnesses (as studies show to be the case in Great Britain), or that, in the Arab world, people had to be certified as reliable witnesses so their worldly-consequent utterances could be given credit in court, or that until well into the eighteenth century parties to a law case in Britain could not also be called as witnesses since their perjury (which was even proposed as a capital offense) was regarded as unavoidable, all suggest that fact-finding is partly about seeking truth, partly about defusing conflict, partly about maintaining a workable sense of one's experience of the world—and all about stitching together law and culture so that each informs and supports the other.

In every instance, too, contemporary peoples are heir to the categories of their predecessors. It thus comes as less of a surprise to learn, for example, that in several European countries (France, Spain, Italy) a defendant in a civil suit can still definitively end the case in his favor by swearing to a fact that would be within his knowledge. While the mode of assigning who may take such a decisory oath in these European countries still depends on whether one is the plaintiff or defendant, in those Muslim countries where this type of oath is employed the court will instead make a determination of who is most likely to know the facts in question and allow that person to cut off rebuttal by taking such an oath. Similarly, legal fictions often betray both the uncertainties of fact in a given culture and the areas where, in return for a desired outcome, a society is willing to leave concepts (such as usury or unjust enrichment) open to interpretation. And where, by design or by circumstance, the "facts" escape whatever form of legal process is applied, cultural assumptions, and often designated experts, may step in to fill the gap.

Law and Cultural Assumptions

The rules of evidence codified for use in American courts are rarely regarded as a document of high humor. But ask yourself if you really think that when people are very excited or actually dying they are most likely to tell the truth, or if in the moments following the commission of a crime your silence means you accept the truth of another's accusation of your guilt. If not, some legal decisions may test at least your sense of humor. So, the testimony of a man who thought he was dying was not allowed because he did not actually expire. And it took a rather droll opinion by the highest court in Illinois to overrule the judge who, in accepting an expletive as equivalent to silence, had argued that since silence refers to nothing and the curse words referred to nothing, the man's earthy response to his accuser was allowable as an admission by silence. (An example, as one anthropological colleague quipped, of the referential theory of language gone mad.) Anglo-American evidentiary rules, which tend to be fashioned as if a jury were present, are not, of course, mere artifacts of the law but reflections of their cultures' assumptions. And we can see how some of these connections operate by looking comparatively at several domains in which such cultural assumptions are at work: in the application of the concept of the self, in the legal assessment of a person's "character," in the development of the idea of intentionality, and in the view of familial relations. An interesting starting point is afforded by the case of Japan.

The stereotype many Westerners have of the Japanese and their legal system includes a strong avoidance of litigation under the pressures of a system of social hierarchy and the desire to maintain social harmony. There is, of course, a fair measure of accuracy in this view: The family as a corporate unit (and the corporation as a family unit), the few number of lawyers, the state imposition of various "conciliation" mechanisms, and the blunt assertion by some local scholars that (as one of them put it) "Japanese do not like law," have, however, been open to reinterpretation. More accurately, perhaps, one needs to think of Japanese disputes as handled by a highly differentiated system in which the idea of the person figures significantly.

"Hierarchy is still part of everyday life in Japan," writes a recent commentator. "It's in every relationship. Whether it's a company, college or otherwise." Indeed, the construction of one's identity is often exquisitely arrayed in such terms. Gifts are always a vital indicator of status, and Emerson's notion that the only true gift is a part of oneself may be, in Japan, something of a non sequitur. In Japan, for example, one needs to know the cost of a gift in order to make a return gift appropriate to one's standing vis-à-vis the other. Stores therefore commonly code items to quietly assist recipients in this calculation. The number of folds in an envelope or strands in the wrapping cord, or the use of odd or even numbers of enclosed bills, symbolizes and enacts the concept that, since hierarchy sustains life, the moral person calculates not personal benefit but alignment with the order of things. The embeddedness of the individual in groupings is reinforced in everything from infrequent personal litigation and judicial pressures toward conciliation to "the absence in Japanese of anything remotely resembling the personal pronoun," as Robert J. Smith puts it. Not standing out from the group and asserting

claims that contravene the social hierarchy contributed to legal forms that have, nevertheless, begun to
change in recent years.

Compulsory conciliation became the favored legal
form in Japan beginning in the nineteenth century,
but conciliation, some Western scholars have argued,
is antilegal: It conduces people to compromise otherwise legitimate claims, it does not build a record of
decisions, and it tends to favor those in power. Seen
from the perspective of many Japanese, however, conciliation forces higher-ranking persons to honor their
obligations, allows people a clear acknowledgment of
their rank, and encourages extralegal pressures. Thus,
notwithstanding increased individuality, the decline
of corporate paternalism, the long delays associated
with a sharp increase in the number of actual court
cases, the risk of being charged costs, and the sparse
number of trial lawyers (there are only twenty-three
thousand lawyers in Japan, as compared to over a mil-
lion in the United States, only fifteen hundred being
allowed to pass the bar each year), most people are
dissuaded from challenging social "harmony" and the
relative certainties of social alignment by asserting
purely legal claims.

In such an environment one can understand the
power of apology, for the nature and degree of humil-
ity both reflect and reassert hierarchical expectations.
By contrast, apology in the West often is equated with
acceptance of liability: Witness the U.S. refusal to apol-

ogize for slavery or the thwarted desire of many of the women involved in the case Judge Lord handled who simply wanted the contraceptive company executives to apologize for the injury done them. Studies show that many Western litigants would be satisfied with some sign of contrition, but the meaning of apology as the public acknowledgment of moral fault—and hence its threat to ideas of equality—is almost the exact opposite of its meaning in the context of Japanese social harmony through social differentiation.

The contrast between Western and Japanese ideas of the person and the Arab perception of the self is equally striking. As we have seen, in Arab societies a person is identified largely in terms of those with whom he or she has established bonds of indebtedness. Since God endowed humankind with reason and one is expected to develop this capacity through attachment to wise teachers and desired connections, the thing one needs to know most, in life and in law, is the relationships someone has with particular others. In the past, courts even had associated with them experts in physiognomy who determined not a person's "character" but whether they really came from the place they claimed to be from and were, therefore, likely to have acted in a given arrangement as the people of that region were known to act. Gender, too, becomes a significant indicator. Men tend to see women as less governed by reason and hence less able to form such prudent ties, but while this "natural" disposition may be a liability, it may also be overcome. Thus, a highly educated woman may gain custody of a child even though strict Islamic law would give it to the husband's kin. Moreover, the idea of the divisible self—one in which a person could play multiple, even contradictory, roles—is unimaginable: Political power is personal, not institutional; judges are never thought to rule contrary to their personal attitudes; property is conceived not as one's relation to a thing but as a set of relationships with others as it concerns a thing; and everyone is expected to use the accepted rules for establishing allies to the benefit of those with whom ties of dependence have been formed. Thus corruption is not the violation of statutory law but the failure to share with those who are obliged to you, and in the constant quest for allies one assesses others for the ways they affect the world of social relations.

When one enters an Islamic court, then, certain procedures can be seen to fit with this idea of the person. Judges usually open the bounds of relevance quite widely as they try to determine what the relationships really are. They would rather set people back to negotiating their own arrangements than enunciate particular rights. Witnesses are gauged as reliable by showing they affect the world of relationships and thus may not be willing to risk the loss of dependents through short-sighted deceit. Knowing a person's "origins"—where he is from and hence his ways of forming ties to others—tells the court vital information, and the idea of not knowing past relationships and acts would, unlike a British or American proceeding, be to deprive the court of vital knowledge. The "facts" are thus filled in more by the appraisal of the person than by observable circumstances, and the experience of human nature and customary social relations suffuse legal thought to such a degree that they are hardly noticed as sources of the law.

What an Arab judge deems indispensable a British or American judge is cautioned to ignore. Unless a party has put his or her character in evidence, Anglo-American law generally precludes its introduction: Past actions—unless habitual or part of the conduct being tried—tend to be excluded. And yet, numerous assumptions and cultural patterns are clearly at work. One might, for example, read the seemingly illogical exceptions to the introduction of character evidence as survivals from some disconnected legal history or, by allowing, say, reputation testimony but not direct evidence of character, as a simple violation of common sense. But one could also see these rules as themselves subservient to the larger cultural concept that holds that, since all men tend to occasional moral lapses, so long as one appears to be struggling against the inner state that yields such failings, legal assessments of char-acter—which the dictionaries say refers to moral quali-ties—must be submerged. Being a moral person is thus largely an interior matter and hence beyond ordinary appraisal. The emphasis on interiority also shows up in particular evidentiary assumptions. In the United States, a nonexpert witness can, for example, testify that someone was "drunk" (even though such an assertion is highly conclusory) because to do otherwise would be to deny that employing that category often *reveals* details rather than obscuring them. However, one may not testify that another was "in love" as that is thought to be so interior to a person as to be unavailable to ordinary perception.

Many Western systems treat the issue of character with notable ambivalence. Take, for example, the case of white-collar crime—the company embezzler, the executive who engages in collusive price-fixing, or the official who loots a company's pension system. Since defendants usually lack a history of criminal conduct, judges tend to focus on awareness of the criminality of their conduct, whether there was a detailed plan involved, and personal motivation as ways of getting at the person's moral blameworthiness. Punishments appear to depend on whether the court believes the person should be held to a higher standard. Rather like a parent punishing a child because, as the child is told, he or she is smarter or better brought up than other children, the punishment may, on occasion, be greater for one who it is thought should know better. Similarly, the consequences of such a person's acts are also of considerable importance to sentencing. (By comparison, it is noteworthy that in many Islamic courts more educated or wealthy persons are often held to a higher standard precisely because the consequences for many others' networks of relationship are thought to be more serious. Sweden and Finland have also issued traffic fines based on one's income.) As concepts of the person change, so too do the ways in which character is determined: In the nineteenth century, as the scientific revolution took on an industrial form, it was thought that character could be determined by measurement of one's face or the bumps on one's head. In the twentieth century, thanks in large part to the psychoanalytic revolution, the assessment of character became a matter of professional competence, just as so much information was being channeled to experts in every domain of life. It may be, as H. Richard Uviller argues, that "today, character evidence most often appears either in burlesque of its function, or as a product of an arcane legalistic wordplay, or as a cruel and senseless shard of forgotten dogma." Perhaps, as a result, the pretense that American juries and judges treat all parties alike by ignoring aspects of character is either a form of hypocrisy that should be faced directly or one of those contested, yet broadly shared, cultural features that people must rely on if they are, quite literally, to be capable of judgment.

On the Continent judges see the accused's past record in the documents presented the court by the investigating magistrate, and while they are not supposed to share this information with the lay jurors who may sit with them, the rule, as one commentator has laconically noted, is not always applied with rigor. Whether the introduction of character information—along with the absence of rules of evidence and the standard of proof as a personal sense of moral certainty—stems from a reaction to the tyrannical use by the ancien régimes of standards that could allow conviction without adequate proof, the result has been to allow professional judges access to such information on the Continent and to preclude it from juries in common-law regimes. Political history, the cultural attitude toward courts and jurors, and the overall perception of persons are obviously relevant to this differential approach to character evidence.

The tensions are clear. Lawyers operating in the Anglo-American tradition compete to add more and more facts, while many of those features by which their citizens normally judge one another are bracketed, evaded, or suppressed. The everyday means of assessment are sneaked in by judges and jurors in an unavoidable attempt to make things seen in court accord with conventional ways of interpreting experience. Appellate courts may refer tangentially to public opinion, the conscience of the community, or—more commonly—just apply their cultural assumptions without articulating them. This is not hypocrisy—though hypocrisy in such matters may, at times, be a virtue—but in the nature of culture, where our sense of the usual predominates lest the world appear far too contingent and chaotic.

One can see many of these elements at work in the fast-changing field of family law. The very idea of what or who is a person has been affected by both technology and social practice. In the United States the question whether a fetus is a person has been at the heart of the religious and political debate over abortion. But it is rendered still more contingent when a fetus may be implanted in a woman who was artificially inseminated, when a pregnant woman loses her fetus to an abusive boyfriend, or when frozen ova may sit in a laboratory while heirs fight over who "owns" them. As is so often the case in Western law, change comes from the margins—whether in claims for the right of homosexuals to marry, in custody decisions when the child was born of an incestuous union, or in the right of a Muslim woman legitimately taken as a second wife abroad to inherit from her deceased husband who moved with his several wives to the United Kingdom. The change in cultural concepts is of necessity one of the most troubling challenges that can be posed for any legal system.

Courts in Iran and the Arab world, for example, that apply a concept of "marital equality" when one person is a ward of the court have had to rethink their categories when someone from a "dirty" trade (like being a mechanic) earns far more than someone from a "clean" trade (like being a cloth merchant). And they have independently developed a concept of the best interests of the child even though Islamic law is clear about the order of custody, since nowadays a woman may be more educated or earn more than the child's father. By contrast, a central African court has held that since women have always been seen as no more competent than children, even an educated woman cannot be treated as a responsible adult or the whole structure of society, the court said, would fail. In the United States, courts that have been called upon to recognize an Indian tribe's right of access to a sacred site have applied a test for what is "central and indispensable" to the Native people's religion, as if the features of dogma, doctrine, and unique sacred shrines applied as universals. Hesse's point that it is in the clash of cultures that true suffering begins is, one might conclude, hardly without its reflections in the law.

Creating Inner States

If concepts of the self deeply affect legal systems, then the nature of people's intentional states presents its own special fascination. Like the development of fact-finding in the Middle Ages or the idea of probability in the seventeenth century, to see how Western, Jewish, and Islamic ideas of inner states affect legal considerations is to gain a unique vantage on the relation of law to cultural history.

Whether the eleventh and twelfth centuries did indeed mark "the discovery of the individual," scholars generally agree that, as part of the monumental changes taking place at this time, a major reconfiguration occurred in the concept of the self. From the time of ancient Greece, when, as Erich Auerbach put it, Homeric man was all foreground and no background, always comprised by what he said and did rather than what he thought or felt, there was no developed idea of the person as having an inner state that might be completely different from what was visible to others. Augustine might speak of an inner self, but even his was not an elaborated set of intentions that might be wholly distinct from what a man does or says—and it was centuries before another writer even attempts a full-scale autobiography. But around the middle of the eleventh century, and through the succeeding century and a half, quite a new set of concepts begins to emerge. Predominantly in the works of men like Bernard of Clairvaux and others associated with monastic orders, there emerges a vision of the self as possessing a separable inner state. This is not the self of modern times—fashioned by the (real or imagined) control of one's own experiences—but a self made possible only through the virtues instilled by God. As the idea of interiority developed, so did the language and examples of its presence. Where once the very notion of *persona* implied a mask that actually revealed the continuity that is not visible on the surface of one's body, Christian thought now bifurcated the self so that one could simultaneously look behind the mask to the features

God had granted men and, at the same time, envision these inner states as possessing attributes that were not in lockstep with observable acts. The result was a gradual spread, from religion to numerous other domains, of the idea of a self not readily apparent to other people and with it the need for a set of terms and devices for getting at this inner state.

As assumptions about the self changed so did the ways in which European legal systems approached the individual. In the course of the twelfth century the idea took hold of an inner self separate and distinct from one's overt acts and utterances. Peter Abelard could thus write to Heloise: "Wholly guilty though I am, I am also, as you know, wholly innocent. It is not the deed but the intention of the doer that makes the crime, and justice should weigh not what was done but the spirit in which it is done." The Holy Inquisition's quest for misdirected choices (the literal meaning of heresy) affirmed the idea that hidden thoughts were beyond its reach, and the church therefore had to develop a way of relating acts to inner states. Even Joan of Arc, convicted in 1431 of heresy, was exonerated twenty-five years later when what had earlier been seen as accessible was now firmly ensconced as visions hidden from the sight of mortal men. As the image of the inner self changed, so too did that of the external body. The body of the king, like that of Christ, became metaphorically fractionated, and metaphors of the state as composed of various appendages, each with its own role,

took on the air of common sense. Laws of strict liability—in which no mental element was regarded as relevant to the defense that might be offered—began to
be replaced by more refined categories of crime that
reflected a person's actual intent. The result of this
florescent idea of the inner self was not, of course, either quickly institutionalized or consistently shared,
but it did start the West down a road with whose repercussions we continue to grapple.

> The thought of man is not triable; the devil alone
> knoweth the thought of a man.
> —C. J. Brian, Court of Common Pleas, 1477

> The state of a man's mind is as determinable as
> the state of his digestion.
> —*Edgington v. Fitzmaurice*, 1889,
>   29 Chancery Division 459

As the heirs to this elaboration of the inner self, we
in the West now take for granted that we do indeed
possess intentions that might be easily misunderstood
if one paid attention only to our actions. One way to
test the relation between commonsense cultural orientations and the multiple domains through which they
gain meaning is to ask how you think your actions
should be appraised in various situations. Ask yourself,

for example, whether you think you should be punished for a traffic offense you did not mean to commit.
If you think that ignorance of the law is no excuse, yet
want desperately to convince others that you are really
a "good person," how would you have us make that
determination? Do you get a different answer when the
issue is whether a man who has sex with an underage
girl should be punished even though that was not his
intent? We may have limited the power of the state by
requiring it to prove a particular criminal intent. And
we may have learned to raise our children by attribut-
ing to them states of mind ("Don't you really love your
little sister?") so as to conduce desired behavior. Inner
state is now crucial to the discourse of most Western
religions, and no novel would ring true if we did not
think we had some access to the characters' inner feelings. As heirs to the language of inner states, we now
accept as given that we can get at such emotions even
as we struggle with the legal and moral implications of
the acts we try to capture in these terms.

Contrast this idea of intent with that found in the
Arab world. There, the common belief is that people
do indeed have inner states, and that such states are
crucial to the meaning of one's acts. The first thing
one does in prayer, for example, is to state that one
has the intention to pray and that one's acts and words
should now be understood only in these terms. But
whereas in the West a gradual fractionation of the self
occurred, in the Arab world the assumption is that, un-

less one is incompetent, a person would not engage in various acts unless he or she had the intent that accompanies them. Thus, Arabs acknowledge the existence of an analytically separable inner state but assume it is accessible if one knows enough about a person's relationships, the contexts that render acts and utterances of consequence in the world. In court, therefore, inquiries about past associations and social background all supply information not just about one's current relationships but one's intent. Instead of having developed a refined language of inner states, however, Arabs have developed a refined set of ways for assessing a person's repercussions in the world, and through them a grasp of one's inner state. Legal method and cultural style here take on a rather different set of implications and connections than in the West, even though each acknowledges the existence of inner states as critical to both justice and common sense.

The cultural history of intent takes a different course in Jewish thought following the destruction of the second temple in the year 70 c.e. With the role of the priests destroyed and the Jewish people dispersed, rabbinical commentaries, refined and collected (most notably for our purposes) in the Mishnah, developed both a style of expression and a purpose that was deeply influenced by the idea of intent. As we will see in our final chapter, Jewish law is as much about creating an orderly universe as resolving actual disputes, and in this process human intention plays a central role. For if one is to fulfill the commandment that one honor God by replicating a universe in which each entity belongs to a given category and holiness consists in maintaining things in their proper category, then it is through what one intends, even more than what actions occur, that the purity of category will be sustained. Whether it is in the determination of what is edible or the separation of clean parts of the body from the polluting, in every domain it is the intention one brings to the effort that determines the categories of the pure. Just as God gave Adam the power to name the creatures of the earth, so, too, he gave humankind the capacity to identify and enact the categories of sanctifying behavior by rendering things according to human intent. If, therefore, one means a permissible use for an object that may otherwise be devoted to impure ends, or if one nullifies doubt by asserting a given purpose, it is by such acts of will that the world becomes a universe of meaning. As Jacob Neusner puts it: "Man by his word and will initiates the processes which force things to find their rightful place on one side or the other of the frontier, the definitive category, holiness."

In law this means that the quest for facts and certainty turns in great part on an investigation of what a given act was meant to accomplish. It was not enough to know *what* had been done; it was essential to know what was intended by it. Deeds have no intrinsic definition: One may not start a fire on the Sabbath, but if one did it to frighten away a thief, its meaning changes; if the object you carry on the Sabbath is thought of as having no consequence, it loses its status as a "thing." As in any such instance a cultural logic fills in the interstices of the unknown. How a single act related to other such acts, how one's whole orientation and history implied a given direction, how the specific act comports with the evidence of its desired goal—all become accessible and indispensable to ascertaining the nature of the situation. A language of inner states thus developed, one that suffused not just the domains of religion and everyday perception but the ways in which one came to imagine that facts themselves were capable of being identified, known, rendered capable of resolving doubt. Intent was not merely a fiction for grasping the unknowable; it was the instrument through which humans, in a divine-like way, actually created the categories of the world and hence what could, in truth, be known.

Intention, it should be noted, may be played up in some cultures and legal systems, but it may also be played down in others. Among the Sherpa of Nepal, for example, it is thought that one cannot grasp another's inner state, and that to try to do so would be as impossible as it would be intrusive, for even though everyone knows such states to exist, any attempt at such an effort renders everyone vulnerable to the manipulative attributions of another. In some societies that have been subject to autocratic rule, those in power have tried to impute certain intentions to their citizens' actions, thus turning the form of opposition into an ill-intended act against society as a whole. And in yet another variant, among the Tongans of the southwest Pacific, even the act of "promising" is regarded as creating no obligation. For them, utterances do not imply intent, and statements about the future are treated as hypotheticals or conditionals. As a result, not only is one not regarded as having breached the possible implications of an utterance by "breaking a promise" but focus is placed much more on other commitments in the ongoing relationship, promise-like statements actually serving to assert that one will not put the relationship at risk by trying to enforce a tie it may prove difficult or undesirable to fulfill.

Indeed, cultural concepts may fill in the facts not only through images of self, action, and inner states but through a naturalized view of human relationships themselves. Take, for example, the question of incest. Often regarded as the one sure universal of human society—which, in fact, it is not—the nearest bounds of incest, wherever a particular society may set them, are commonly felt with such intensity as to seem incapable of being arbitrary human creations. Theories meant to account for this taboo include those emphasizing the need to marry out or die out, the biological repugnance of having sex with close relatives, or the sociological need to differentiate specific roles. That each of these theories is flawed in no way alters its local importance or the fact that, within any grouping, the bounds of incest change in response to other cultural and social factors. In Britain and the United States, for example, until well into the nineteenth century, marriage to a sister-in-law was regarded as incestuous. Rumors of such a desired relationship nearly ruined Charles Dickens, while the allure of this relative was neatly expressed in one version of the final stanza of "My Darling Clementine": "So I kissed her little sister / and forgot my Clementine." To this day, roughly one-third of the American states regard first-cousin marriage as incest, while the remainder do not. There are, then, "facts" that may appear imminent at one moment or place only to be altered completely in the light of changing social circumstances.

By contrast, other facts, known to be of human construction, may nevertheless appear to be sufficiently based on nonlegal sources that they too take on the air of the apparent. For example, in the United States the laws that govern what happens to the property of one who dies without a will are said to represent what people would have done had they but expressed their desires. In almost all of the states the pattern of the intestacy law is to propel property down the generational scale rather than to allow it to return to the parental or grandparental generations. When asked, most people say this is quite "natural"; one study showed a strong preference that such laws disinherit even mothers to the advantage of a spouse. For those who live in extended families or come from a different cultural heritage, however, such assumptions may not reflect their view of familial relations, and (wills aside) they may have their own mechanisms for constraining a different form of sharing the belongings of the deceased. Whatever the pattern, two features are especially striking: that the process is almost always characterized in naturalistic terms, and that the connection of law to assumptions about kinship, even when outdated or unrepresentative, is felt with almost visceral attachment rather than being regarded simply as a matter of administrative choice.

The relation of fact determination to emotion (if one may put it that way) is also exemplified in those situations where people "feel" they know the right answer even when they cannot articulate it. It may be that, as Roy Wagner has said of culture generally, "The things we can define best are the things least worth defining." Or it may, for example, be that the legitimacy of an arbiter is undercut when he or she tries to give greater specificity to a proposition than accords with ordinary experience. In any event, the articulation of the inarticulable presents itself in many legal situations, of which several drawn from the realm of pornography law may be seen as exemplary.

In the British case of *Shaw v. Director of Public Prosecutions* the Lords upheld the common-law misdemeanor of conspiracy to corrupt public morals as applied to a charge of publishing an illustrated directory of prosti-

tutes. Most of the judges argued that jurors can tell
when something is so objectionable that it outrages
public decency, and that such a concept is not so vague
as to be unenforceable. A similar example comes from
the American jurisprudence on pornography. In 1964
Justice Potter Stewart, after a careful analysis of the law
on the subject, concluded by saying of pornography
that even though he could not define it, "I know it
when I see it." Commentators have either dismissed
this remark as mere dictum or tried to rationalize it in
the context of the full opinion as a deeply reasoned
argument. While "strict constructionists" like Justice
Scalia may emphasize rule-based rather than case-by-
case reasoning, and others argue that passion has a
proper role to play in adjudication, perhaps a more
cultural approach would be commended by Occam's
razor. For if the categories a judge applies are embedded in the assumptions of their culture, then what is
happening is not, as Karl Llewellyn suggested, either
"unconscious" or "intuitive," but the expression of just
those typifications that hold a world of experience sen-
sibly together. To "know" pornography when you see
it or a drunk when you encounter him is not to enact
some mechanical cognition that everyone in a culture
shares in exactly the same way; rather it exemplifies
the need to unpack the categories of which that conclusion is composed in terms of the symbols and domains through which their very movement grants
them the power of the obvious.

Filling in the Facts

Cultural assumptions fill in the facts in numerous ways. The demeanor of a witness is said to be crucial to most Western legal proceedings—for determining truthfulness, no less than propriety—and toward this end judges and jurors may look at a person's "body language" as an index of deeper attitudes. Yet the ways in which even the same orientations may be displayed obviously vary enormously from one cultural or subcultural context to another. In the novel *Snow Falling on Cedars* the situation is put quite dramatically when a Japanese-American tries to display himself with the rigorous control of emotions that, in his subculture, indicates maturity and veracity, only for the American jurors to interpret his stoicism as a sign that he is heartless and insincere. The same may be true for speech styles. Studies have shown, for example, that American women commonly use, among other features, a rising tone at the end of statements or a tag question ("Isn't it?") that jurors (at least in simulation exercises) often take as indicative of a degree of uncertainty. Are women, being relatively weak, taught from childhood not to seem too assertive, and do they therefore tend to conduce acceptance of their assertions by appearing to get men to actually confirm the content of their utterances? Do they use the same style in conversation with other women to create solidarity? If a speech style grounded in the distribution of power in the culture has the repercussion of making women appear less certain, and hence less credible to an inquiring policeman or court of law, the process may be so subtle, so implicit, so insidious, and so poorly appreciated that the connections between law and culture require the most thoughtful analytic and practical consideration.

So how to explain his face to people? He had meant to project to the jurors his innocence, he'd wanted them to see that his spirit was haunted, he sat upright in the hope that his desperate composure might reflect the shape of his soul. This was what his father taught him: the greater the composure, the more revealed one was, the truth of one's inner life was manifest—a pleasing paradox. It had seemed to Kabuo that his detachment from this world was somehow self-explanatory, that the judge, the jurors, and the people in the gallery would recognize the face of a war veteran who had forever sacrificed his tranquility in order that they might have theirs. Now, looking at himself, scrutinizing his face, he saw that he appeared defiant instead. He had refused to respond to anything that happened, had not allowed the jurors to read in his face the palpitations of his heart.
—David Gutterson, *Snow Falling on Cedars*,
   1995, 154–55

Of course, one "solution" to the uncertainty of fact found in numerous systems is reliance on the opinions of experts. Their roles may take many forms. When special groups of merchants or community members are impaneled, the institutionalization of expert knowledge may be very direct; when counsel for each side commences the "battle of the experts," one may be forgiven (to borrow a phrase) for wondering how those not qualified to serve as experts nevertheless get to judge among them. Experts are called by the court in civil law jurisdictions, rather than by the adversaries as in common-law countries. But the claim (as, for example, in the "cot death"/sudden infant death syndrome cases in the United Kingdom) that it is preferable to use only a list of approved experts ignores the fact that each will still speak from his or her own theoretical orientation regardless of who brings them to court. (What Disraeli apparently said, it should be recalled, was not about statistics, but that "there are lies, damned lies, and experts.") An average of four experts per trial appear in over 90 percent of all civil trials in the United States, while scientific experts appear in every case involving product liability. Experts in the social sciences, to come closer to home, have testified on an extraordinary range of issues, including the meaning trademarked words have for ordinary consumers, the probability of a child growing up to be a juvenile delinquent if placed in a given custody situation, and the reaction an Indian caste member may have to rejection by a co-ed at an American college. These experiences have, in a number of instances, not only had a significant effect on the development of some legal systems but on the theory of the discipline from which they originate.

In 1972, for example, the United States Supreme Court decided that Amish parents did not have to send their children to school beyond the eighth grade as required of all other students in the state of Wisconsin. At the trial, anthropologist John Hostetler testified that "if the Amish are forced to attend school against the religion of the church-community, and to remain in the school teaching values contrary to their belief, great psychological harm can be done to the children." Indeed, he argued: "I think that if the Amish youth are required to attend the value system of the high school as we know it today, the church-community cannot last long, it will be destroyed." Characterizing the testimony of the defendants' experts as "uncontradicted" and "unchallenged," the Supreme Court repeatedly noted that the Amish were law-abiding farmers who were no burden on society: The ruling in favor of the Amish parents tracked much of the anthropologist's testimony. The majority spoke of the danger to the whole community of the loss of some of its members; the dissent by Justice Douglas picked up on Hostetler's own published figures showing some communities lose up to half of their members yet obviously survive. It is particularly interesting to note that Hostetler's claim that the community was at risk of destruction is itself grounded on a highly questionable functionalist theory. It assumes that a society is like a clockwork mechanism or an organism, and that if one part of the society is adversely affected, the whole structure may fall apart. Had other experts been presented who used a theory based on culture as a set of contested symbols, or societies as constantly evolving, both the chosen facts and the emphasis placed on the expert's opinion may have been quite different.

The reciprocal effect on anthropological theory of involvement in the legal process is well represented by the role scholars have played in a number of cases involving American Indians. In 1946, as part of its program to terminate the distinctive legal status of Native Americans, Congress passed legislation allowing suit against the government for past actions that harmed the Native peoples. However, only a "tribe, band, or other identifiable group" was permitted to bring a case before the Indian Claims Commission. But how were these terms to be defined, and how was one to prove a particular group fit the definition? Anthropologists became deeply involved in the process and were themselves forced to go back to their own ideas about tribes in the process. Thus, the ideas Julian Steward incorporated in his book *A Theory of Culture* were, like the work of many of the more evolutionary or historically minded anthropologists, a direct outcome of their involvement in these proceedings. Similar reactions have arisen from such cases as the Mashpee claims for

Fig. 11. Black children with white doll, 1942. (Photograph by
Gordon Parks, courtesy of Spencer Museum of Art, University of Kansas, Museum purchase: Friends of the Art Museum.)

the return of land in the late 1970s and the still more
recent use of anthropologists in attempts by previously
unrecognized tribes to gain federal recognition. One
could point to analogous cases in many other places
in the world, from land claims by Australian aborigines
to the characterization of group rights among the Sami
(Lapps) of Scandinavia.

Some uses of expertise have become particularly notorious. The U.S. Supreme Court's reference in *Brown
v. Board of Education* to the tests done by Dr. Kenneth
Clark, purporting to show that black children had a low
opinion of themselves because they chose white dolls

Fig. 12. Mistaken conviction (Robert Buckhout, "Eyewitness Testimony." *Scientific American*, December 1974, 23–31.)

over those that look like them, contributed to the resistance southerners demonstrated to the Court-ordered desegregation of public schools. Similarly, the studies and testimony of psychologist Elizabeth Loftus have raised very serious questions about the accuracy of eyewitness identifications. To some the standards for admitting scientific evidence—based on a controversial array of criteria about methods, standards, and relevance to the facts at hand—call into question the credibility and usefulness of non-laboratory-based disciplines. And when experts play a key role in the "scientific" selection of jurors—as in the conspiracy trials of the Vietnam War protesters, the Rodney King and O. J. Simpson cases, and a number of high-profile commercial and corruption trials—their perceived effect on legal proceedings may call into question the very legitimacy of the entire jury system. In at least one instance, the role of an expert witness has actually proved fatal. Nikolai Girenko, who had appeared in a number of court cases to testify about skinheads and other racially motivated hate groups in Russia, was shot dead in June 2004, the "Republic of the Russians," a neofascist group, having claimed responsibility for the act.

> One of the most humiliating moments in my career as an expert came when I caught myself changing my outfit over and over again before a human rights hearing, thinking all the while about how best to satisfy law's desire. Should I wear a dress? No, not academic enough. Should I wear a jacket? No, too masculine. Did I own any items of clothing that were sufficiently authoritative but still non-masculine? . . . [L]ike a rape victim . . . I then realized I was not just an expert; I was also an exhibit. . . . My own experience of law shows that at least in some instances law acts not as a sovereign but rather as a seducer whose ability to generate willing, loyal and even loving subjects lies precisely in "formalities," in technical rules and unspoken agreements to preserve law's illusion of autonomy simply through acceptance of rules not only of procedure but also of decorum.
> —Mariana Valverde, "Social Facticity and the Law," *Social and Legal Studies* (1996): 213–14

Yet expertise itself means different things in different situations. In Islamic law, reliance on local experts (to establish the level of support appropriate for a wife of a given status, for example, or the regional customs associated with ways of forming contracts) must be seen as part of the mechanism for keeping power dispersed and bringing local matters to the court's attention. Indeed, since being an expert, whether of a craft or of the law, is regarded as consistent with the proposition that there is no distinction in Islamic society except as to knowledge, the whole meaning of developing one's capacities for social advancement is inseparable from its manifestation in each institutional domain. By comparison, the meaning of expertise has probably changed in American society over the past half century: As crosscutting ties within the community decrease, there is ever greater willingness to find some expert— on education, happiness, health, or language—who can substitute professed stature for that of earlier relationships. In each instance, "facts" may be determined through deference to these experts, but the very meaning of their roles and their claims will be deeply suffused by the meaning that expertise itself has garnered in other contexts of social and cultural life.

Conflicted Culture

Throughout much of the generation that began in the 1960s many cultural anthropologists operated with a theory that characterized culture as "shared symbols."

It was an enormously productive concept, one that came to have a profound influence on other disciplines—literary studies and history, in particular—as it validated the ability of each to reach across disciplinary boundaries and include as legitimate sources of information such previously denigrated data as that concerning nonelite actors or unwritten accounts. For anthropologists, the theory clearly placed the stress on the second of these components, the nature and action of symbols. The contribution of ideas and theories this emphasis produced were extraordinary: If thought is carried by symbols, it becomes possible to unpack the structure of these symbolic forms and get at the ways in which collective ideas and actions are oriented; if symbols are transformed, even reversed, in various rituals or spatial arrangements, forms of dress or food categories, one has readily to hand an instrument through which one can get at some of the mechanisms through which a society is, quite literally, cobbled together. And if one now takes as one's domain nothing less than all the ways in which a people manifest the categorization of their world, all sorts of possibilities present themselves for theorizing about just those issues with which earlier theories had such difficulty— how change may occur through the medium of metaphor, how the domains of men and women may in some cases appear to be radically different yet qualify as transformations of the same components, how the disorientation or collapse of an entire society may be engendered by a loss of symbolic meanings.

But if the "symbols" part of this equation was given prominence, the "shared" part got rather less attention. By the 1980s, perhaps as the political and academic environment in the West had undergone its own changes, it was precisely the shared aspect that began to appear problematic. How, people asked, can one really say that the powerless share the culture of the powerful under whose dominion they live; how can we even refer to this process as "sharing" when individuals quite obviously read different meanings into every social and legal concept imaginable, from the meaning of *art* or *moral* to *rights* and *person*? New theoretical questions arose from this questioning: How much and in what ways must people actually share orientations in order for us to speak of them as living in the same society or culture; is "passing acquaintance" or force of circumstance sufficient to keep a society together; and how can a legal system be said to possess legitimacy if a large part of the population subject to its processes and assumptions does not possess the same basis for accepting its legitimacy? Words once more current in philosophical discussion began to creep into legal matters, words like *indeterminacy* and *open texture*. Perhaps because many scholars felt the times warranted less certainty or because minority voices were becoming more audible, scholarship, not surprisingly, followed the crowd.

Once again, the results have been mixed. New voices have indeed been heard, and even if concepts like "subaltern" or "praxis" will become quickly dated, the

quiet assumption that, at least at some critical level, all
the members of a culture accept the power of their
concepts or the natural quality of their institutions has
been aptly disrupted. As with so many ideas in the sciences and social sciences, though, ideas do not get dis-
proved so much as they cease to generate new debate
and insight, and while the problems they posed remain
unsolved, the scholarly caravan, no longer able to
rouse itself to a sense of the new, moves on. That many
ideas may, for example, be "essentially contested" and
that whole cultures may be fashioned on such a notion
rather than the definite structures posited by earlier
theorists is far from being a trivial point. But without
such ideas garnering further investigation or hypothe-
ses, it is easy for them to go unnoticed. In legal studies,
the idea that all is not shared is a point anyone who
hangs around a criminal court for an afternoon might
have appreciated; that it has only produced the realization that the rich and the poor do not, in fact, sleep
under the same bridges renders further consideration
along these lines rather banal.

More circumscribed inquiries, however, do partake
of this general question of the shared, and in that respect the results, if themselves contested, have not
been without merit. Consider several examples drawn
from the social and legal issues surrounding indigenous peoples. Suppose a plant is found on the lands of
a native group that exists nowhere else. What "rights"
should the native peoples have in it: Should they be

able to copyright or patent it, should they be able to cut others off from its beneficial medical uses? If we think of the issue in property-like terms, how far will we extend that concept: Can I sell parts of my body or rent my womb or get a trademark on my genes? If we put the matter in terms of rights, and if we think of rights as an indeterminate concept that can and should be suffused with multiple meanings, perhaps we can apply our cultural theory—which suggests that concepts must reach out into various directions so as to fulfill their adaptive capabilities—and thus see our legal approach as gaining truth not from certainty but from agreement on the process of momentary formulation. Or if, to take another example, we define a tribe not by specific features of descent or territoriality but as an amoeboid entity whose critical feature is not its shape but its ability to shift shapes, then we might grant legal recognition to claimants even though their tribe seems to appear and disappear over time rather than maintain a constant identity. In each instance, the question of the shared, the nature of the symbols as vehicles for maintaining orientations, and the reconceptualization of time as revealing of process rather than truth offer the possibility for theoretical and practical insights unlike those afforded in the past.

Legal systems, then, must indeed create facts, but they do not do so in isolation. Indeed, for all their attempt to appear definite neither the principles a system embraces nor the procedures it affects are any less

concrete for possessing the very qualities they embody,
like all cultural artifacts, of felt specificity in a framework that is quite open-textured. The development of
the jury in England or the management of doubt
among Islamic law scholars, the precipitation of a concept of an inner state and the assumption that people
tell the truth in extremis are all instances of orientations attached to particular institutional structures.
These structures absorb and radiate meaning precisely
because they connect the features of their people's
lives through sufficiently clear symbols, sufficiently
shared as to render everyday life, for those who en-
twine themselves in its terms, adequately meaningful.

CHAPTER 3

Reason, Power, Law

> Analogies can decide nothing, that is
> true, but they can make one feel
> more at home.
> —Sigmund Freud, *Introductory
> Lectures on Psychoanalysis*

Moving Metaphors

Imagine what a difference it makes if one thinks of the heart as a pump rather than a furnace, the eye as a receptor rather than a beacon, the atom as the irreducible unit of matter rather than a miniature planetary system. Imagine what it could mean to a program of research if one thinks of the relation of the egg and the sperm as an act of conquest or as one of attachment, of viruses as warriors or as part of a system of locks and keys. Consider the impact of viewing the market as governed by an "invisible hand," one's body as a "temple," language as a set of "games," society as an "organism," a "code," a "text," or a "field."

Metaphors are the glue of social and cultural life: They knit together the different domains in which our concepts and our relationships exist with such force that they seem to be features of the natural world. This joinder of the known and the unknown is quite wonderfully captured by the Modern Greek word *metaphora*, which actually refers to a moving van—a vehicle that carries you from one settled spot to another! Indeed, metaphors may be our species' vehicle for keeping open the possibilities of moving from one way of conceiving reality to another, of adapting to changing circumstances by keeping alive the very mechanism through which conceptual alteration is effected. Not surprisingly, then, the choice of metaphors also possesses moral overtones: Does it not affect one's obligation to an outsider if one takes to heart the statement in Genesis: "A stranger shall you not oppress for you know the heart of a stranger, since you were strangers in the land of Egypt." As Cynthia Ozick has said: "Inspiration belongs to riddle and oracle; metaphor belongs to clarification and human conduct." Notice, too, how difficult it is to find an alternative metaphor when one has taken hold—how hard it is to think of consciousness except as a "stream," time as "flying like an arrow," or dangerous speech as akin to "shouting fire in a crowded theater." Try to operate without metaphors and watch yourself bumping into them at every turn— a doubly difficult prospect since, in most instances, the power of metaphors lies in no small part in their seeming perfectly obvious.

What is true in every domain of culture is, by definition, true in law as well: Do you agree that the test of race or gender equality depends on "a level playing field," that freedom of expression operates in a "marketplace" of ideas, or that welfare statutes are valid as a "safety net" but not (in the phrase of one U.S. senator, no doubt trying to attach welfare to luxury and laziness) as a "hammock"? If you think of a copyright as being like a parental interest in your "brainchild," you may require a different level of creative input than if you think of it as a "property." And if you decide the custody of a fertilized ovum implanted in another woman on the basis of who has contributed most to the child's creation versus who "owns" the ovum or intended to "have" the child, you might get very different results. Whether a legal system explicitly relies on metaphors or implicitly works through analogies to recognized legal categories, metaphors serve as a vital bridge connecting the style of legal reasoning to a society's overall style of cultural reasoning.

In many legal systems, of course, reasoning styles have developed in ways that appear highly distinctive to the legal domain itself. The categories made available to decision-makers, the analogies that one shares with colleagues, the need to mask the substantive through the technicalities of the procedural may all contribute to a style of logic that separates law from an ordinary citizen's idea of commonsense reasoning. Yet, in the view of some, like Richard Posner, there really is no such thing as legal reasoning, in the sense that one cannot point to a formal set of logical principles that link decisions to one another: Beliefs about abortion or the death penalty, he asserts, "live below reason and are no less worthy for doing so." Other, more functionalist, arguments are founded on a different emphasis: that a shared style of reasoning enables agreement on specific issues where complete agreement on theories is not possible, that a shared reasoning style corrects biases in individual judgments, or that basic agreement on a mode of reasoning (like rules of the road on the highway) makes other actions possible even though they are themselves mythologized as immanent. Seen from a cultural perspective, even those systems that possess intensely technical and professional qualities, or that speak of themselves in self-serving terms of rationality rather than an arguably more realistic language of power, nevertheless betray, at a broader level, those features of logic and sociologic without which their utterances would be neither comprehensible nor accepted. The contrast between common-law systems and several others once again provides an entry point to such an understanding of legal reasoning as cultural reasoning.

It was Edward Levi who argued that the common law works by a series of "moving categorizing concepts": By looking at similar cases the judge derives a general precept that is said to apply to or distinguish the case at hand. In that sense it is really a later court, by matching previous decisions to current concerns, that says what the earlier decisions "really" stand for. Thus the categories set up by one court on the basis of its reading of prior decisions may, in turn, generate additional categories, while continuity appears to be maintained as each new instance is subjected to a similar mode of incorporation or distinction. Levi's view may be seen as a prescription for orderly change or as a rationalization of the historic and political process through which the substantive rights of the few are preserved through the procedural demands applied to all. Either way, one can test Levi's interpretation of common-law reasoning through its connections to the style of reasoning found in the surrounding culture.

Note first that Levi's formulation stresses the fact pattern through which analogy proceeds. Over the course of Anglo-American history those of us who employ its style have come to imagine that we are exceptionally good at determining "facts." Whether such an emphasis is related to the political move that strengthened the individual against the state—so that the state had, in criminal law especially, to meet the heavy burden of proving both the external facts of a matter and the internal state of the accused—or is related to the developing idea of the individual as a free agent leaving the traces of his will in a moral and commercial universe of his own contracting, the idea that events and persons could be discerned from features in the physical world came, particularly in the course of early modern times, to inform religion and literature no less

than philosophy and law. With the gathering legitimacy of the scientific revolution the idea, as we have
seen, of degrees of moral certainty was married with
the world of material evidence, and the law followed
other cultural domains in gaining great confidence in
its ability to ferret out such "facts." Similarly, the particular form taken by British individualism stressed the
role of the person over that of the category, emphasized that causation implies agency rather than mere
chance (such that fault implies moral failing more
than simple accident), implied that change was
equated with moral development (which, like the common law, was itself a perpetually incomplete act), and
furthered the idea that power could be dispersed to
local decision-makers who would (like the oracular
jury) pronounce on the facts while leaving ultimate
power in the control of state appeals. Even time—seen
as linear, progressive, fulfilled by nature and nature's
God—came to suffuse the common law, rendering
precedent simultaneously cumulative and reversible,
the embodiment of an orderliness that is at once immanent and controllable.

So great is the cultural belief in discernible "facts"
that in modern times many Western systems seek expertise about virtually all occurrences—from tire
tracks or blood types to hair samples and DNA—and
are reluctant, even when the statistics are clear, to
apply, say, the distribution of death penalties by race
in America when "the facts" do not prove them to

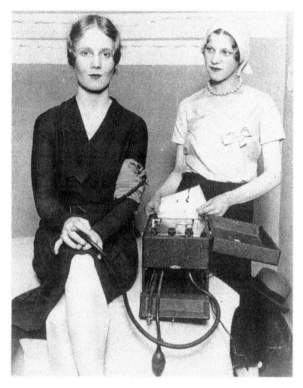

Fig. 13. Advertisement for an early lie detector machine.
(University of Iowa Libraries.)

apply to a specific case before the court. Although
courts have yet to accord legal value to lie detector
tests, many law enforcement agencies obviously believe
in their efficaciousness. It is unlikely, however, that
many of them know that the first such machine was
invented by a Harvard-trained psychologist, William
Moulton Marston, who was also the creator of Wonder

Woman, the comic book heroine whose magic lasso could make anyone tell the truth! That we tend to believe such machines possible underscores our commonsense commitment to such a perception of "facts," a perception that is itself reinforced by being replicated in so many different cultural domains.

Compare this, once again, to what takes place in Islamic law. There, I would suggest, courts imagine themselves to be exquisitely adept at perceiving persons, rather than facts. Not only is the use of circumstantial evidence relatively new and rare but the common emphasis continues to be on understanding who a person is—who he is related to, how he has dealt in other contexts, and what sort of network he currently possesses. Thus a court will ask questions about one's background or past acts that an Anglo-American court would regard as irrelevant or unfair. Judges even claim (as one Saudi high court judge put it) that "I can always tell if a man is lying once I know his background and relationships." Muslims sometimes criticize Western law by saying, "How can you have a fair proceeding without knowing as much as possible about what a man has done in the past?" In most Arab variants of Islamic law this emphasis is wholly consistent with those cultural emphases that also seek knowledge of a person's traits and ties wherever they appear, as well as with the view that power is intensely personalistic rather than institutional, that time represents sets of relationships rather than a directional stream of events, and that causation (whether religious, political or legal) should be traced to some sentient being more than to the impact things may have on other things. The result is a style of analogic reasoning that favors what might be called a moving system of categorizing "persons" rather than the Anglo-American form of categorizing "facts"—a style that, as we would expect, manifests itself in virtually every other domain of Arab culture.

Reasoning Styles

Legal systems, as we have seen, may possess family resemblance even if they do not constitute a taxonomy that tracks precisely the reality of the physical world. In this sense the variation in Western forms seen in civil and common-law reasoning may be instructive. The temptation, of course, is to fall into one of the many stereotypes continentals and common lawyers, each seeing the other as "an imperfect approximation of himself," have hurled at one another across the Channel for centuries. Thus British lawyers (say the continentals) are incapable of abstract thought, that continentals (the common lawyers retort) have been mindlessly seduced into a naturalized view of legal categories embraced in codes, and that (as everyone can

shamelessly allege) each of these legal orientations really stems from some ineradicable flaw in the other's
national character. Even so learned a scholar as R. C.
van Caenegem asks if civil law is authoritarian and
common law democratic, and gives a resounding yes
to the former question and an only somewhat more
equivocal yes to the latter.

> The common law expands from the facts. The
> civil law, for its part, would as soon *forget* about the
> facts. It qualifies them (that is, it subsumes them
> within legal categories) and rapidly proceeds to
> address the question whether this or that provi-
> sion of the civil code (or other legislation) ap-
> plies, what its meaning is, what the impact of a
> given interpretation of this provision on other
> dispositions of the code will be, etc. . . . [T]he ci-
> vilian is preoccupied with order . . . while the
> common law judge persistently operates at the
> level of the messy facts; she is concerned with *dis-
> order.* . . . Unlike the civil law, which seeks to *appre-
> hend* legal disputes through a complex categorical
> design of hierarchical norms purportedly com-
> prehending all eventualities, the common law
> *awaits* the interpretive occasion. It is reactive and
> not, like the civil law, proactive or projective.
> —Pierre Legrand, *Fragments on Law-as-Culture*
>   (Deventer: Willink 1999), 76 and 69

> In Germany, under the law everything is prohib-
> ited except that which is permitted. In France,
> under the law everything is permitted except that
> which is prohibited. In the Soviet Union, every-
> thing is prohibited, including that which is per-
> mitted. And in Italy, under the law everything is
> permitted, especially that which is prohibited.
> —Newton Minnow, former chairman of the
>   U.S. Federal Communications Commission

More usefully, one might try to connect styles of
legal reasoning with other aspects of political culture
and history. For example, the assumptions that may be
operative in a given legal system may, as Pierre Le-
grand suggests, embrace styles of moral inquiry that
are characteristic of other domains of the culture. European civil law systems may do more than find the
right code provision to match with a given case: The
need for direct oral confirmation of any evidence, the
opportunity to tell one's story without constant interruption, the presence of lay jurors alongside the state-
appointed judge, and the open-ended evidentiary process—in which many aspects of a person's life beyond
the strict confines of the case are thought vital to understanding who this person is—are all statements of
moral expectation. The same is true for a common-law
proceeding, in which facts that do not bear on the case

in question are regarded as totally irrelevant: To regard as not relevant what a person has done in other
circumstances is no less a moral statement than is the
reverse process in civil law systems. Where facts in European systems are subsumed in the extant range of
categories, in common-law cultures the emphasis on
differentiable facts appears to connect with a style of
moral assessment that leads to categories being
formed *from* instances rather than through their discovery *as* instances of prior categories. And while the
concern of the civil law may focus on the threat of disorder, the concern of the common law may be with too
centralized an order. Anglo-American styles of reasoning may, as Sir Henry Maine indicated, secrete their
substantive propositions in the interstices of their procedures, while the moral and cultural style of Continental cultures may fabricate a sense that one must
focus simultaneously on the categories of the code that
give structure to relationships and a clear assessment
of who the person before the court really is.

In each instance, cultural orientations that lie beyond the law are crucially supportive: the European
history of securing the individual against the depreda-
tions of the state by raising state institutions to a level
of impersonality and "scientific" truth, and then protecting the individual through law as an arm of that
state; the British emphasis on "possessive individualism," the sharp separation of public acts from private
morals, the emphasis on "practicality" as a surer test of

worth than being true to form, and the elaboration of the idea that change—whether dangerous or beneficial—comes largely from the eccentric. It is not some imagined "national character" that is at work in each instance, but a complex mix of cultural categories and their articulation in a system that can be regularized and appears to operate by standards that are broadly consonant with the style of reasoning and values of society at large.

Indeed, anthropologists, confronted with remarkably different styles of cultural reasoning, have raised the question whether people in different cultures actually reason in fundamentally different ways. Like philosophers and linguists they often come to this question having encountered seemingly bizarre modes of putting experiences of the world together. Among some of the people of New Guinea, for example, animals are categorized according to their odors, while meat and vegetables are grouped by the way they feel in one's mouth; among many African groups only the emanation of witchcraft could truly explain the occurrence of various events, while for the matrilineal Trobriand Islanders it makes sociological sense that men are seen as largely irrelevant to procreation. Similarly, as we watch Western legal systems grapple with religions that have not previously been part of the cultural mainstream—such as those of immigrants or indigenous peoples—we sometimes see the courts trying to understand whether, say, a belief in voodoo is tantamount to provocation when the "victim," however "mistakenly," believes his life to have been in danger. We have known at least since Durkheim that our forms of social organization correlate with our images of the inchoate: As Marshall Sahlins quips, when we were pastoralists God was our shepherd, when we became monarchists he was enthroned as our king, and now that we are proper capitalists he keeps track of us through double-entry bookkeeping. But the "rationality debate," as this issue has sometimes been denominated, itself often seems to turn, ironically, on a kind of category mistake: The issue is really about how people put categories together, not whether they are "wired" differently, and legal reasoning, even in its most professionalized versions, must, therefore, tap into the recognizable modes of a culture's reasoning for at least a portion of its legitimacy.

How reasons are given in legal systems may, then, reveal much about the institutional history and the cultural meaning of which they partake. Appellate decisions in the United States, for instance, are expected to be detailed and relatively transparent. Dissenting opinions are not only published but may eventually be adopted by later courts. On the Continent, by contrast, published opinions are very short, rarely relate the "facts" in the case, and seldom reveal disagreements among the judges. It is not that the former are better reasoned than the latter; it is that the expectations— based on the assumed role of the courts, the use of codes versus previous opinions, and the image of law as less dependent on personal assessment than imminent categorization—connect to issues of legitimacy in quite different ways in the two types of systems. Perhaps no domain is more revealing in this regard than the role of jurors.

Juries and Reason

Juries, of course, have many forms and quite diverse histories. We may tend to think of them primarily in terms of the Anglo-American form, and, as we have seen, the divergence of fact-finding mechanisms that occurred in the wake of the abolition of the ordeals is crucial to the story. Juries may also seem to be increasingly irrelevant inasmuch as they have all but disappeared from civil proceedings in Great Britain and the percentage of jury trials in the federal courts of the United States has declined in the past forty years from 11.5 percent of all civil cases to 1.8 percent, and from 15 percent to less than 5 percent of all criminal trials. In 1961 India, having deemed them a failure, eliminated juries altogether. One American judge has commented that what we are seeing is "nothing less than the passing of the common law adversarial system that is uniquely American." But since the rules of evidence largely operate as if a jury were present, since the impact of the jury on the popular imagination remains critical, and since many state and national cases operate in the shadow of a potential jury trial, their role in the United States and elsewhere remains, like the miner's canary or an indicator species, an important sign of the culture of law as a whole. Even in countries influenced by European laws jurors (commonly referred to as "lay jurors") are also frequently present, sitting alongside professional judges in many proceedings, usually without any special capabilities, though in a few instances (as in Finland) in a quasi-professional role. In recent years we have also seen the experimental introduction of juries in countries as diverse as Spain, Morocco, the nations of eastern Europe, Russia, and (beginning by 2009) Japan. Because detailed studies of the actual operation of juries are largely limited to the experience in common-law countries and the mixed panels of western Europe, it is to these examples that we will turn for insights into the nature of their reasoning processes.

Common-law juries give no reasons for their decisions. While jurors in the United States may speak to the press following a decision—as opposed to the British practice, which, since 1981, treats such disclosures as contempt of court; the French, which requires lay jurors to swear never to disclose anything about their deliberations; or the Brazilian, where jurors vote by secret ballot without ever deliberating—there has never been much of an effort to require demonstrations of

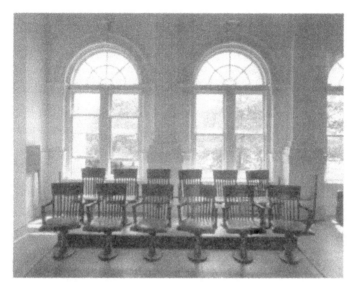

Fig. 14. Empty jury box. (Photograph by Jim Dow, Grady
County Courthouse, Cairo, Georgia, 1976–78. Seagram
County Court House Archives Collection, Library of
Congress.)

the bases for jurors' decisions. To some this is consonant with the political role of the jury: As the almost
disembodied pronouncement of "the community," juries speak with a single voice whose oracular quality
serves, in a positive sense, to mystify their utterance.
Others, noting the absence of articulated reasons,
count it as beneficial that jury silence relieves the state
of blame for the decision, and that it encourages the
jurors themselves to greater efficiency and courage. It
may also be difficult to ask amateurs to formulate a
unified set of reasons. Whatever qualities the jury may

possess in theory, however, our understanding of actual jury decision-making remains largely secondhand: When, in the 1950s, Congress learned that permission had been granted to secretly record jury deliberations for an academic study, the legislators immediately passed a statute against such eavesdropping and impounded the existing tapes. Thus much of our knowledge of these matters is based on impaneling mock juries and studying how they decide cases. The results have nevertheless been quite fascinating.

For example, it has been argued by a number of those conducting such studies that American jurors do not, in fact, simply listen to the evidence and then retire to the jury room to sort through all of the data to reach a collective decision. Instead, jurors put together a narrative as they individually listen to the trial, matching each new piece of information to the story they have been telling themselves along the way. As they view the entire body of evidence and begin to discuss the case among themselves jurors work towards a collective narrative, one that necessarily depends on the ways in which narratives are generally created in their culture. So, for example, the story is told chronologically, "facts" are related to worldly consequence, and character is evaluated on the basis of implied criteria of causation and explanation even if no such evidence was offered. Faced with the unusual context of collective decision-making, it appears that jurors treat with equivocal perception what they take as given in everyday life: In fashioning an outcome it is only after they have reached their decision that they grasp what it was based upon, discovering, as it were, the situations in which they are acting only after they have acted on their orientations. Proceedings in American small claims courts, where people generally speak for themselves, may, however, flounder as a litigant's common-sense relation of the story departs from the legally adequate way in which, for instance, agent and cause must be connected if liability is to attach.

As jurors seek their footing the very idea of how truth is thought to emerge in a legal proceeding reveals much of its attachment to views of human nature and political history. In common-law countries one talks about how "truth emerges from adversity," an image that has deep reverberations in religious ideas, educational models, political campaigns, sporting events, and one-on-one narratives of personal heroism. The adversarial trial, as a story told about the human situation, is thus a reaffirmation of—indeed a vital contributor to—a vision of the nature of truth and the human condition. By contrast, in France a witness is allowed to tell his or her story without interruption, the inquiring judge being better positioned, it is thought, than contending counsel to eventually get at the truth. Indeed, in Western cultures truth is commonly imagined as "straight" rather than "crooked," where for the Barotse, who fully expect that people will lie, the truth is said to meander back and forth before arriving at its goal, "like cattle moving towards water." Under certain circumstances even Westerners may, however, tolerate a nonlinear story: As one commentator has put it, "we can tolerate the justice in factual ambiguity, in reasonable doubt, as long as we locate it in a tale that lets us feel certain about something—even if it is only the certainty that we are heroic in resisting temptation to yield to a false certainty."

In voicing his own skepticism of jury decision-making Judge Jerome Frank argued that since jurors might reasonably disagree about the facts, reason cannot possibly be the basis for their judgment. But that misses the point: A cultural style of reasoning, whether by jurors or judges, may be constructed such that different interpretive outcomes are indeed possible even while the mode of working through them remains characteristic. The style may be like that of a chain story, in which each new relater adds something distinctive yet the comprehensibility of the whole is rigorously maintained—like an innovative utterance that is nevertheless grammatically correct ("twas brillig . . ."). Small wonder, therefore, that when Thomas Kuhn came to formulate his ideas of paradigm shifts in the structure of scientific revolutions he should have analogized them to common-law legal reasoning, where normal interpretation must at times yield to conceptualizations that better suit changing perceptions. Perhaps, too, we can see why the reasoning process of the jury is not necessarily irrational if it fails to follow the direction set out by the court in its final charge, since most charges have been shown experimentally to be confusing at best to the jury. Instead, the style of reasoning tracks the assumptions and orientations the jurors bring with them from their shared and diverse cultural backgrounds. Nor should it be so surprising to learn that complex litigation, which may have absorbed months of testimony, is not altogether elusive to jurors inasmuch as they continually revise their appraisal in the light of an ongoing narrative. Similarly, the assessment of expert testimony, so crucial in many American and British trials, seems to depend greatly on the culturally distinctive ways of attending to another's believability rather than on the evidence alone.

Thus comparison suggests that while the particular form any style of legal reasoning takes is necessarily distinctive, in each instance the link between cultural and legal reasoning is quite evident. When, for example, the Moroccan government introduced a jury system for certain cases in the late twentieth century, it turned out to be an interesting failure. According to those who participated in some of these trials, the fact that jurors could not engage the parties to the case in direct conversation was tremendously frustrating. These jurors told me that it was not possible, without having such interpersonal contact, for them to determine if the person was telling the truth. And if one watches the ways in which Moroccans assess others, this is perfectly comprehensible: They simply must engage the other in direct discussion if they are to feel they have the information they need for appraising him. In the absence of such a relational mechanism jurors found themselves at a loss to decide many cases, and the whole experiment was abandoned.

Other examples are equally intriguing. Very few trials have been held before juries in Spain since the reintroduction of juries in 1995, but the requirement that they give a brief rationale for their decisions, coupled with indications that submitting detailed lists of decisional points to the jury only confuses them, may suggest that, once again, culture and legal expectations may not—perhaps purposely—have been rendered compatible. Similarly, it remains to be seen whether the bar to mentioning a defendant's criminal record or introducing evidence of good character will accord with the average Russian juror's sense of what is needed to render a commonsense decision as that country, too, experiments with Western-style juries.

Among the cultural assumptions that may affect legal reasoning are also those that relate to ordinary ideas of probability. Formal probability, as we have seen, is a development of the seventeenth century in the West, and in many other cultures of the world the assessment of events continues to be drawn in terms of authoritative opinion or a strict dichotomy between occurrence and nonoccurrence. But where the idea of probability has taken hold, its appraisal, as part of its integration into a broader cultural pattern, has developed certain aspects regarded as commonsensically true. Thus in a famous American case a jury was asked to find a defendant guilty because the statistical chance that anyone else would fit the description was said to be astronomically high. Put in the extreme such arguments seem appealing: How likely is it that anyone other than the defendant, like the perpetrator identified by witnesses in a hypothetical situation, would also be a midget who wears bloused combat boots and a nun's habit while riding a candy-striped pogo stick and smoking a banana? When individual features are simply multiplied to produce one-in-a-million claims, statistics can be very misleading. Such misuses of statistical analysis aside, commonsense probability may be unavoidable in any legal process since judges, jurors, or arbitrators will inevitably draw on their cultural knowledge (including its assumptions about correlations) to determine the facts. If, in short, those appraisals are based on the belief, say, that women are by their nature less perceptive than men, or that men are unlikely to know about women in the way that midwives or matrons do, the outcome will necessarily vary with the beliefs that inform it.

Similarly, appeals may be made, directly or indirectly, to public opinion. In the early nineteenth century Chief Justice John Marshall, for example, was extremely clever in his reference to public opinion when addressing the legal situation of the Cherokee Indians. Mindful that a very large proportion of the American population opposed the efforts of the states (and, eventually, President Jackson) to remove the Indians to the west, Marshall drew on his brilliant command of the language to counterbalance claims of American sovereignty with the sensibilities, as he saw them, of the American people. With ringing phrases and striking analogies he fashioned a way of bringing public opprobrium into a situation in which, in any strictly legal sense, it would have to be regarded as irrelevant and prejudicial.

> The title by conquest is acquired and maintained by force. The conqueror prescribes its limits. Humanity, however, acting on public opinion, has established, as a general rule, that the conquered shall not be wantonly oppressed, and that their condition shall remain as eligible as is compatible with the objects of the conquest. . . . [As] they are incorporated with the victorious nation . . . the new subjects should be governed as equitably as the old. . . . When the conquest is complete, and the conquered inhabitants can be blended with the conquerors, or safely governed as a distinct people, public opinion, which not even the conqueror can disregard, imposes these restraints on him; and he cannot neglect them without injury to his fame, and hazard to his power.
> —Chief Justice Marshall, *Johnson v. McIntosh*, 21 U.S. (8 Wheat.) 543 (1823)

A corollary of attending to public sentiment consists of focusing the process of legal reasoning on the definition of the situation. Sociologists who use this concept generally mean that, among the range of alternative interpretations of a given set of "facts," people of diverse orientations within a single culture may negotiate, from their respective positions of power or belief, over the way all parties ought to categorize the situation. So, for example, a psychiatrist may effectively require a patient to accept that the situation is one in which the patient bears the primary responsibility or fault as the price of the analyst's assistance; or a client may be expected to accept the lawyer's view of fault rather than the client's own if the lawyer is to be willing and comfortable offering professional advice. Similarly, triers of fact or arbitrators may expend much of their efforts on negotiating a view of the situation—asking, for example, whether the case is about "privacy" or the public interest, or whether this is a situation of familial rights or the right of the state to assert its values—rather than on some supposedly mechanical application of established juridical principles. How the situation is defined is itself the cultural prerequisite to establishing what might be done about it. And where some legal systems may act as if this process of negotiating the situation were not really taking place, others (such as Islamic legal systems) have institutionalized the inquiry in ways that are utterly consonant with the same process of negotiating those social ties

that characterize both their way of interacting with others and their way of imagining an ordered universe.

Discrepancies may, of course, exist between those
who are formally endowed with the power to operate
the legal system and those who move in and out of it
with no professional attachment. Although one could
point to those who urge extrajudicial settlements as a
way of opposing state power or act out of their religious
roles to assert values they find lacking in formal proceedings, perhaps the most striking example of con-
testing formal legal power is to be found in the process
of jury nullification.

Already by the thirteenth century in Britain we have
documents showing that jurors would not support the
requisite legal remedy when they found it either too
harsh or based on assumptions they did not share. Because they did not have to give reasons for their actions, any more than do contemporary jurors, medieval juries could effectively nullify the existing law in
particular cases. In Britain and the United States, the
process of jury nullification has both political and social aspects. In 1670 a British jury refused to convict
Quakers William Penn and William Mead of unlawful
preaching. The judge locked the jurors up for the
night without food or drink or "so much as a chamber
pot, though desired." When the jury refused to alter
its verdict, they were fined: It took a higher court's
order for them to be released. (In 1989, in what might
be a modern version of such a situation, a judge in

Pittsburgh, exasperated with a verdict he called a "travesty," sent the jury home without paying them for their five days of work.) Similarly in the early days of the American republic the refusal of a jury to convict newspaper publisher John Peter Zenger of seditious libel effectively ended such prosecutions, while during the period of the industrial revolution jurors repeatedly refused to find in favor of railroads under the then current doctrine that workers had assumed the risks of their occupation. Eventually, legislation caught up with jurors' attitudes. During the Vietnam War jurors repeatedly found the government's charges of conspiracy against war protesters too vague to warrant support, and, although the law was quite clear, the refusal to convict sent an unequivocal message of its own. Indeed, when O. J. Simpson's attorney was allowed to appeal to the jury to "do the right thing; you are [he concluded] the conscience of the community," was he, in effect, asking them to place the need to send a message to law enforcement about racism over the need to decide the case on its merits? In a 1997 Colorado case a juror was actually convicted of contempt and fined twelve hundred dollars for telling her fellow jurors they had the power to nullify the law—even though she had not been asked about her beliefs during the voir dire. Some cognitive psychologists have argued that jurors do not nullify the law unless they have already perceived unfairness as a result of their assessment of the defendant's appearance or de-

15. Chicago Seven jury, drawing by Ben Shahn (© Franklin McMahon/CORBIS)

meanor, their categorization of the person within society at large, or because they perceive judicial bias.

Two centuries ago jurors could actually be told the implications for punishment of their verdict, which sometimes resulted in them convicting the defendant of a lesser offense in order to avoid a harsh result. Indeed, jurors until recent times were often instructed that they were judges of both the facts and the law. Only a couple of states still allow such a charge to the jury. A fringe political movement, associated with other antigovernmental programs, continues to assert that the constitutional power of American juries to decide the law is a right that must be restored if one is to achieve a genuine government of limited powers. Legislators in some parts of the United States have introduced bills to inform jurors of their right to decide the law because, as one of them stated, it is necessary to protect minorities against "lopsided law enforcement" and because "the law has gotten away from the average person." Since a 2004 decision by the Supreme Court holding that jurors, not judges, must decide if each element of a crime has been proved, why, even some scholars have asked, should a jury considering, for example, a case of petty theft not be told that if this would constitute a third conviction for the defendant it would automatically trigger a life sentence? Sir William Blackstone (1723–1780) wrote, "It is true, that the mercy of juries will often make them strain a point, and bring in larceny to be under the value of twelvepence, when it is really of much greater value: but this is a kind of pious perjury, and does not at all excuse our common law in this respect from the imputation of severity, but rather strongly confesses the charge." Similarly, modern opponents argue that the result of granting juries such powers, in the words of one federal judge, "would be chaos and lawlessness."

Obviously any such discussion of the jury necessarily trenches, therefore, on the broader issue of the distribution of political powers. The Tocquevillian view that the jury is vital to participatory democracy or the populist argument that juries are the best agent for bringing the moral into the realm of the legal remain at the heart of the American (and, to an extent, the British) perception of power. Obviously, that participation is affected when only about one-third of those called for jury duty in the United States ever show up at the courthouse. The new jury system in Japan will incorporate a fine for jurors who avoid their civic duty or reveal the details of a trial. Scholarly findings, political perspec-

tives, and perceptions of jury rationality also have a tendency to get inextricably tangled. "Behavioralists," who
frequently rely on laboratory experiments of dubious
methodological value, see jury decisions as unpredictable and would defer to a paternalistic state operating
by more "rational" economic criteria. Opponents
worry that all the errors of the law-and-economics
movement would simply be imported into the realm of
the jury. Politically there are also significant contrasts
between American and European mixed panel juries.
Studies show that many of the twenty thousand jurors
who serve each year in France are skeptical of the rep-
resentativeness of their selection even though recent
reforms broaden the base from which they are drawn.
Nullification is not unknown: As one French juror told
a researcher, "The law is badly made, aberrant, and we
had to vote against what we knew to be true to reach a
verdict in which we believed." Perhaps the absence of
a specific level of proof, other than the culturally laden
idea of "following your conscience and your inner conviction" (to quote the French Code of Criminal Procedure), plays some role here. And while a number of
American judges actually claim that jurors undergo a
kind of emotional transference, becoming captivated
by the court, French jurors, rather like the German lay
jurors studied years earlier, express a not inconsider-
able level of willingness to disagree with the judge.
Americans have never revolted against the government they formed, and even though they consistently

express broad confidence in the state, they remain highly skeptical of allowing control to get very far beyond the local. Europeans, Latin Americans, and many Asians, by contrast, are more openly skeptical of the state, including the judiciary, and do not seek an image of themselves in its processes.

> The jury, and more especially the civil jury, serves to communicate the spirit of the judges to the minds of all the citizens; and this spirit, with the habits which attend it, is the soundest preparation for free institutions. . . . It teaches men to practice equity; every man learns to judge his neighbor as he would himself be judged. . . . The jury teaches every man not to recoil before the responsibility of his own actions and impresses him with that manly confidence without which no political virtue can exist. . . . By obliging men to turn their attention to other affairs than their own, it rubs off that private selfishness which is the rust of society. . . . The jury contributes powerfully to form the judgment and to increase the natural intelligence of a people; and this, in my opinion, is its greatest advantage. [F]or however great [the juries'] influence may be upon the decision of the courts it is still greater on the destinies of society at large.
> —Alexis de Tocqueville, *Democracy in America*,
>   vol. 1, Vintage edn., 1960, 291–97

Before the tribunal retires to deliberate, the presiding magistrate shall read out the following direction, a copy of which shall also be displayed in large print in the most conspicuous position in the retiring-room: "The law does not require the judges to give the reasons which persuaded them, and it does not lay down rules governing the sufficiency and weight of the evidence; it requires them to ponder intently, in silence, and to ask, in all sincerity of consciences, what impression has been conveyed by the evidence adduced against the accused and by the defenses presented by the accused. The law requires the judges only to answer this one question, which embodies the sum total of their duties: Do you have that inner conviction?"
—French Code of Penal Procedure, art. 353

Each of these political and cultural factors contributes to the acceptance or skepticism expressed about the processes of legal reasoning. Have lawyers, in the name of fairness, made the benefits of law available only to those who share their place in the class structure? Has the very language of the law rendered claims to reason so far removed from the social and economic bases of actual decision-making as to undermine belief in the legitimacy of the law itself? Or have various systems constructed their forms of legal reasoning—like their forms of cultural reasoning—so as to allow a common conversation to continue, to allow disagreement over results without destroying the shared acceptance of a mode of analysis, and in the process replicated the cultural style of coherence through structured ambiguity, passing acquaintance, or even "a kind of half-acknowledged cultural fiction that retains a much greater power than many a self-evident truth"? Indeed, may it be that law, as a mechanism of ordering relationships, does much of its work not simply by making disputes represent a culture's way of analyzing people and their attachments but, at least as significantly, by creating a sense of the orderliness of the entire cosmos? It is to this topic that we may now turn our attention.

Law and Power

Law may be about reason. But it is also about power. Power may take any number of forms—from sovereign command and brutal force to subtle social pressure and appeals to apology—but the effects will be deeply entrenched in the overall structure of power through which that society enacts its cherished values or the interests of those who possess control. For the student of law and culture examples of the interplay of power, reason, and law suggest connections that, if one's concerns stop with issues of efficiency or doctrinal law, may elude notice.

We have already seen how, in the course of British legal history, the use of indirect control allowed the Normans to implement their domination of a conquered people. During the height of the colonial period the British continued this theme in such diverse places as East Africa and the Indian subcontinent. Thus British officials effectively created bodies of Muslim and Hindu law, and while allowing these partially indigenous legal regimes to apply in their own courts, the invocation of the repugnancy clause—that no law could be repugnant to "justice, equity, and good conscience"—constituted, as appeals to Westminster for the appropriate writ or higher-court ruling had done since medieval times, a check on the free development of such local laws. But as in all cases of legal imposition, the effects were reciprocal. Just as slave-owners were affected in their music, cuisine, and genes by those subject to their control, so, too, the colonial powers were not left without influence by those subject to their dominion. It is a story as old as Rome, as recent as the judicial assessment of a Native American religious belief that the exercise of power over another is not without its influence on the conqueror.

Indeed, the example of Native Americans and the law is a fitting instance. From the first legal decisions in the early nineteenth century, when American law had to conceptualize a people who were neither the equivalent of foreign nations nor states, the deep-seated ambivalence Americans have always possessed towards their indigenous population showed itself in legal dealings. So while tribal sovereignty was conceptualized, in part, in terms of conquest and discovery, courts also recognized that Indians also possessed a degree of sovereign control superior to that of states themselves. A tribe's right to be governed by its own rules thus includes the power to treat male and female members of the group differently despite the fact that, as American citizens, gender equality ought otherwise to apply. The Indians' powers may be limited in a variety of ways: Congress and the courts have "plenary power" over American Indians and have frequently imposed conflicting policies on them; when Native rights are seen by some whites as amounting to "special privileges," a backlash of legislation and local nonenforcement frequently sets in. Yet the overall ambivalence about Native Americans in the country's history and consciousness cannot be left out if a full understanding of their legal and cultural story is to be understood.

Power and culture come together in analogous ways in the field of family law. Here, the fundamental question, from a practical and philosophical point of view, has to be: What business is it of the state to intrude into what are, after all, quite private arrangements? Indeed, it was not until the late Middle Ages that marriage became a sacrament for the church, not until early modern times that marriage became firmly embedded in state, rather than religious, institutions, and now that nearly half of all couples in most European countries—the figure is even up to one-third in Catholic Ireland—do not bother to get married, it is problematic why the state should be involved in these personal relationships at all. Without considering how the ideas of individuality, the legitimacy of state sanction, and the very meaning of family are undergoing profound change in society the legal repercussions become incomprehensible.

One form of power that frequently escapes notice is the power to control the terms of the discussion. Many who grew up under Nasser say that no Egyptian could use terms employed by that charismatic leader without the overtones he had given them. Similarly, when a Supreme Court justice speaks of a "clear and present danger" or how an act may "shock the conscience of the community," far more is created than a legal concept. Few courts can simply enforce their decisions by constantly sending out the police to do so: Rather, much of the enforcement comes through citizens accepting the terms of the discussion as set down by those in authority. The language may fail of its purpose—desegregation, famously, was supposed to occur "with all deliberate speed"—or it may become the common coin of the culture—competition must occur on "an equal playing field." But the power of words is invariably part of the equation of power, and legal systems—however institutionalized, however separate from state control—are nothing if they are not forums for capturing the terms of discussion.

Legal domination and legal alienation occurs, too, when people cross cultural boundaries, when they have little connection to the way a host country has come to adopt its rules, or when they feel that the rules of their home countries hold greater legitimacy or practical necessity. Israeli Arabs, for example, commonly get documents in Jordan as well as Israel to back up their arrangements, and Palestinians will commonly secure a marriage by referring in the bride-wealth transfer to the site of a home now located in Israel. Muslim women from North Africa usually get documents relating to divorce or custody back in their native land, and not just from a European court, believing the former to have greater meaning and effect in their own community. And when disaffected Muslim youngsters who have grown up in Europe are discriminated against by European laws or practices and teased in North Africa for their poor knowledge of Arabic, it is little surprise that they should frequently remark that "we are homesick everywhere." While it is imperative to study such legal alienation, it is equally important to recall that such alienation is part of a larger pattern and that having pointed to it is not the same as having given an adequate account of it.

Finally, in a world of transnational movement and cross-border transactions it is still an open question whether international law will simply be the law of the powerful or whether, indeed, local practices working around the edges of the formal law will be of far greater import. Many business agreements now incorporate by reference the law of England or an American state as governing in the event of a dispute. But that may only mean that trade arrangements, based on nonlegal ties, will become all the more important, or that allowing a Western nation's law to apply in the business realm will actually give greater scope to the use of local laws for matters of criminal or family law jurisdiction. Whatever the results, studies of history and culture suggest two factors that are likely to remain extremely important in the face of seeming globalization: the local always has a way of reasserting itself as people keep responding to the cultural imperative of category experimentation, and the changes will be reciprocal despite the seemingly incommensurate array of powers. To ignore these factors is to risk, as scholars and as practitioners, some very big surprises.

CHAPTER 4

Law as Cosmology

> How, given what we believe,
> must we act; what, given how we act,
> must we believe?
> —Clifford Geertz, *Local Knowledge*

Putting Things in Their Place

How do you feel about eating a dog? Oh, I'll make it quite appetizing: Puppy-burger on pumpernickel (hold the mayo); fricassee of Fido, with three different kinds of sauce. If you come from a culture in which dogs are eaten with alacrity, particularly if they are thought to have medicinal and restorative powers, you will have no problem—unless, as in Seoul in 1988, you close the dog-stew shops so those attending the Olympics will not think you barbaric. If, on the other hand, such a meal is unimaginable, then learning that you had inadvertently eaten a dog may literally cause you to be sick to your stomach. Since puppies are no more inherently cute than a lamb, a calf, a chick, or a bunny rabbit—which you might eat without a second thought—something more than nourishment is obviously at work.

Ask Westerners why they do not eat dogs and one reason they are likely to give is that a pet is like a member of the family—and eating family members is wrong. (After all, 84 percent of American dog owners refer to themselves as the animal's mom or dad, while 43 percent actually celebrate their pet's birthday with a wrapped gift!) And if the human propulsion to categorize means anything, it surely implies distinguishing, say, incestuous partners from those with whom sex or marriage is possible, separating those who possess spiritual powers from those who lack any sacred qualities, and differentiating those who are edible from those who are not. Mixing categories characteristically implies danger, impurity, humor, or madness. Hair on your head is fine, hair in your soup is not; menstruating women may disempower men or pollute the sacred; holding a business meeting while talking like Donald Duck is either funny or nuts. Much of the work of society and culture consists of distinguishing and organizing categories in order that the world make sense and operate as it should. Law, once again, is deeply enmeshed in this process.

But there may be more to it than that. Law, like other cultural domains, may not merely contribute to category formation and regularization; a key role of most legal systems, quite apart from addressing disputes, consists precisely in their ability to help maintain the sense of cosmological order. When anthropologists talk about cosmology, of course, they are not referring specifically to the physical structure of the heavens—though that will certainly be included—but about the entire realm of experience as a unified and sensible whole. Since cultures are systems, not random collections, of diverse domains and the concepts that bind them together, we stay close to the meaning culture confers on our lives when we cleave to its integrative claims. If the categories by which we grasp the world actually maintain our world, and if, in the legal realm no less than many others, long-term order may be accompanied by a sought-after short-term disorder, then it is at the point where boundaries are delineated that the telltale role of law as cosmology may be most readily apparent. Consider, in this regard, the cultural defense plea and the incest taboo.

A series of actual cases will help set the stage: Believing her husband's extramarital affair to have brought intense shame on her family, a Japanese woman residing in California kills her two children and attempts to take her own life. Certain that another Haitian's practice of voodoo is a direct threat to his life, a man strikes and kills his adversary. A Puerto Rican threatened by other Latinos in his Connecticut community goes home for a gun and when he is confronted again, instead of running away as the law requires and believing no one in his community would have anything to do with him if he acted otherwise, he shoots one of his antagonists. Thinking the birthday party for an American's thirteen-year-old son is a proper occasion to test the boy's transition to manhood, a Cambodian man, drawing on the practice of his own culture, grabs at the boy's genitals, only to be charged by the parent with child molestation.

In every instance, the accused claim they are not only remaining true to their cultural roots but that to do otherwise is to require them to give up their culture or to expect them to make choices that are not realistically available to them. At the very least, they argue, the meanings of their acts are incomprehensible—and any punishments meted out would be unjust—without appreciating this cultural background. The 1994 acquittal by a Paris jury of two Africans who admitted violating French law by having their daughters "circumcised" may represent an instance of both nullification and a belief in the relevance of culture to an understanding of the act itself. The West African mother living in Britain who cut scars in the cheeks of her son as part of their tribe's ritual of manhood was found criminally liable, but is she not without some justification in claiming discriminatory treatment inasmuch as Queen Elizabeth II was not charged with a crime when she had Prince Charles circumcised? Like the Australian aborigine who killed the woman who referred to his genitals, you cannot, these defendants say, hold them to a standard of behavior without comprehending, from their perspective, what it was they were doing.

If the world makes sense in terms of the standards of one's culture, it is difficult not to consider cultural background even if one does not defer to it. When the American court releases the Japanese woman for time served if she gets psychiatric help, does it not project its own cultural assumptions about human motivation? (Or, as one wit put it, in America the insanity defense *is* our cultural defense.) Understandably, one may feel that the price of immigration is that one must obey the laws and customs of the host country. But don't you want to know what each of these people meant by what they were doing, even if you do not want to allow a formal defense based on culture? And is it not often the case that it is when we are most threatened with a world that seems to be falling apart that we rely on the most normative, indeed the most traditional, ways we have learned to play our roles and keep the universe together? Allowing a cultural defense may be like allowing any other novel defense: It may introduce a new paradigm that reunites concepts that have been fractionated by instances that prior ideas have been increasingly unable to contain. If so, one can see in these cross-cultural conflicts that it is not only political and legal conflicts that go unaddressed: Such instances also pose a challenge to the way the world itself makes sense.

Or take the example of incest. Theories for the incest taboo come in various forms: that the kids will look strange, that if people don't marry out the group will not forge the alliances it needs to survive, that there is some innate physical or psychological aversion to sexual relations among those attached by kinship or residence, or that roles need to be differentiated so that no one is his own uncle or grandfather. The problem, of course, is that none of these theories is fully satisfactory on scientific grounds. Inbreeding would have to be intense and long-term to yield disproportionately deleterious effects, alliances are achieved without having to marry out, people in states that bar first-cousin marriage hardly possess instinctive repulsion while the folks across the border who allow such unions exhibit no such promptings, and roles can certainly be segregated irrespective of sexual relationships. Indeed, we have instances of societies where no incest taboo exists at all—as among the Na people of China—and it goes without saying that different societies draw the boundary for incest in radically different ways.

But there is one other argument that the members of any culture can make, one that concerns cultural identity: We are the people (they may say) who do not eat dogs or marry our cousins, and we have every right—to say nothing of every need—to maintain these practices as one among many ways we identify ourselves to ourselves and others. The results may be enabling or discriminatory, but their integrative power is ignored at one's peril. Thus, to complete the example, the lines of incest will necessarily connect with numerous practices crosscutting all sorts of domains—property holding and inheritance, religious images and the division of labor—and the maintenance of such boundaries through legal and cultural enforcement is integral to maintaining a sense of the orderliness of the world, not merely avoiding or resolving differences.

Working the Cosmos

Indeed, as we have already seen the predominant point of some legal systems may be the maintenance of cosmological sense rather than "practical" dispute resolution. Two examples are worth noting in this regard, those of Jewish law and Tibetan law.

Jewish law of the Mishnaic period, as we have seen, starts from the supposition that it is the human power to create categories that fulfills God's intended purpose. Reasoning operates by posing examples that, while they may seem so unreal as to be outlandish, actually serve to hone and enact the vital requirement that one attain purity by discerning and maintaining the proper categories into which all things should fall.

Unusual examples test this capacity. Thus the rabbis may ask: If the fruit of a planted tree may not be used for a specified number of years, how does one count time for a transplanted tree? If the active ingredient in a medicine happens to have been extracted from a pig, does it lose its "pigginess," and hence its impure quality, by being reduced to a chemical compound? And (perhaps most wonderfully), if a man falls out of a window and lands on a married woman, thus impregnating her, have they committed adultery? It is not, of course, the situations per se that are the issue: It is using such cases to demonstrate that the law is part of the entire process of being holy by maintaining a world in which things are true to their kind.

Jewish law of the Mishnaic period thus assimilates facts to settled categories; Anglo-American common law allows facts to forge a shift in the categorizing concepts; Islamic law, deferring to the local version of what facts mean to people's relationships, allows facts to speak to their consequences through local custom, personnel, and standards. Where Mishnaic thought marshals legal reasoning to the creation of pure categories, Western common law reviews the facts of the current case in the light of arguably analogous situations, while Islamic law adduces an acceptable view of the implications of a case for social order by applying the culturally recognized rules for legitimization by personal persuasiveness. In each instance, the sense of order in numerous other domains is linked to law as one of the mechanisms that is itself constitutive of that very order.

A somewhat different emphasis is exemplified by Tibetan law. Tibetans, at least in the period before the Dalai Lama fled to India in 1959 in the face of Chinese incursion, saw the world kaleidoscopically, as a place in which patterns emerge and change, in which (as Rebecca French has analyzed it) "the practical present, the known past, the Karmic future" move from coherence and momentary existence to incoherence and cyclic reformulation. Buddhist precepts suffuse the style in which disputes are addressed no less than any other domain: Radical particularism conduces to assessing each case distinctively, moral suasion takes precedence over the attribution of rights, reasoning eschews dichotomies in favor of creating civility in the face of inherently indeterminate relationships, and the absence of closure accords with the legal goal of calming the individual mind. Tibetan life thus possesses meaning only through its rootedness in the larger cosmological order. By replicating this hierarchy and the distribution of social power in the domain of the contentious, law becomes an exemplar of cultural forces rather than some exquisitely separable part of it. As in many African and aboriginal societies, law treats the ailment that disputes are said to engender in the social body and thus keeps the entire cosmos functioning in a healthy way.

> Disputes and crimes are looked on as sicknesses
> disturbing the proper functioning of the social
> "body" ... they do not call for authoritarian
> solutions; conflicts, when they occur, must not be
> resolved, but "dissolved" by conciliation proce-
> dures. In all circumstances the essential is to re-
> store harmony, for harmony among men, linked
> to the harmony of the cosmos, is something
> which must be ensured if it is desired that the
> world live in peace according to the natural order.
> —V. C. Igbokwe, 1998

Similar examples arise in other forms of Western
law. If we return to the example of contract law, we can
see, for example, that a transition occurred from such
elusive notions as a "just price" to the idea that contracts were made when independent wills converged
to a "meeting of the minds," a vision that was consonant with changing ideas of the individual and of the
elaboration of moral worth being demonstrated more
by choice than by ritual correctness. Form contracts
thus constitute an intriguing test of alternative cul-
tural/political approaches: American law remains uncertain about how to treat such unbargainable terms in
the light of the dominant paradigm of free negotiation
and individualistic agreement, whereas the European
approach (as a uniform statute puts it) provides that
no term in a standard contract that the other party

"could not reasonably have expected" will be enforced, the social value of protecting someone suffering from the "asymmetry of information" taking precedence over the image of the person imagined as truly free to make any choice and responsible for its consequences without state protection. To enforce a contract as a way of reinforcing the commonsense understanding that people may not unilaterally impose obligations on others or because society requires people to keep their promises is to couple law with assumptions that reverberate in everything from weekly sermons to philosophical discourse.

Science, too, may add its legitimacy even when it is actually in service of assumptions that have no demonstrable foundation. In the 1970s, for example, as American women increasingly sought careers yet had to cope with the potential guilt of not adequately attending to their children, an article was published in a scientific journal claiming that if women immediately established physical contact with their babies, they could insure the mother-infant "bonding" that is vital to proper child development. The "science," however, turns out to be completely fallacious. The argument seemed to make sense, however, because it assuaged the possible guilt of career mothers with the ring of scientific truth. (Incidentally, it was also possible to buy a "male nursing bra" into which two bottles could be placed so the father could also bond with the child!) In a custody proceeding, then, would someone who had "bonded" with her child be more likely to win custody? Was the standard that applied for custody determinations through the 1970s and 1980s in the United States—that custody should go to whoever is the "psychological parent"—based on genuine science, or was it, in a country that had taken aboard Freudian thought as an entire cultural idiom, a professional viewpoint that could now be raised to a legal standard? Compare each of these examples to the innumerable ways in which we find legal "facts" more believable if they are backed by science or expert testimony. One may, therefore, fairly ask: Is the science serving legal determinations, or is the law's use of science reinforcing and legitimizing social arrangements more generally?

An equally revealing example comes from the field of criminal law. The development of the idea of kleptomania is actually tied up with the development of the department store. In the latter part of the nineteenth-century women became the primary consumers for the household. However, a respectable middle-class woman should not simply be walking around on the street, even if she were shopping for her family. Hence the department store had great appeal as a place where one could be inside, seen by everyone else, yet go from one kind of shop to another without having to simply walk the streets. The only problem was that some women began pinching things. These middle-class women could not, however, be treated like common criminals. So the entire issue got medicalized: Such women were said to take things because of a physical condition, one that actually came to be localized as a problem with the womb. The solution was to send them off for various forms of medical treatment. Since men had no wombs they could not be kleptomaniacs. And to this day, if one goes to the desk manual for psychiatric diagnosis (DSM-IV), kleptomania will be found listed as an ailment that "appears to be much more common in women."

That such an interpretation could take hold in the late nineteenth century made perfect sense given the tendency at that time to medicalize all sorts of issues. This is also the period in which male circumcision, for example, becomes common in Britain and America. In what can only be described as an atmosphere of antimasturbation hysteria, Victorians assumed that if a boy rubbed his foreskin against his penis he risked going blind or crazy, and therefore the best solution was to remove the foreskin altogether—even at the risk of seeming to be like a Muslim or Jew, hardly a sought-for identity. It is a little-known fact that even in Britain and America in this period women who were thought to be too highly sexed were subjected to operations to remove a portion of the clitoris. That male circumcision is still thought to be "healthy" (when there is very little evidence to support that view, and some to the contrary) and not an example of child abuse, and that female circumcision is thought to be unconscionable (when even Western scientists debate its effects) only underscores the ways in which the medicalization of sociocultural assumptions may become the common sense of the law as well.

Representing Justice

Justice, to soften a phrase, is a veritable courtesan among concepts. If we remember how we have been slighted more vividly than how we have been praised, if we counsel sweet reason when it happens to another and lust for revenge when it happens to us, or when, from that moment in kindergarten when everyone was punished for what one person did, it is probably our sense of justice and injustice that will be keenly aroused. As with any other idea that comes embedded in emotion this concept must have some definite form; like any cultural concept, it has to be poured into some vessel to have shape and meaning. The representation of justice, in deed and word and symbol, becomes a condensed instrument for the expression, and hence the deciphering, of a sentiment that reveals many connections in a sociocultural system. Among the places where we can see these inchoate ideas of justice at work are in spatial arrangements of the forum and the iconic representations of Justice as a human or divine figure.

The cosmological appeal of law is made manifest in the rituals and representations of the law. If one looks, for example, at the physical arrangements of legal decision-making forums—whether a meeting of villagers under a tree in the marketplace or litigants arrayed before the courts of the land—one can see this quite strikingly. In American jury trials the judge, dressed in a black robe, sits on a raised bench, counsel alongside their clients, and the jury in a box to the side. In Britain, the judge, still commonly dressed in a wig, sits even higher than his or her American colleague, looking down on the jury, to whom he is later permitted to comment on the weight and believability of the evidence in a way that would be quite shocking to an American judge. In criminal proceedings, the defendant is brought up from the lower floor directly into the dock without being seated next to his lawyer. The prosecutor, who may be the defense counsel in another case, sits closer to the opposing lawyer. In France, the criminal procedure code requires the jurors to sit alongside the judges if the courtroom architecture permits it, a configuration that lawyers claim has a major effect on the dynamics of the trial. And in Germany, where lay jurors sit alongside the judges, a former prosecutor told me that they were taught that upon entering the courtroom they should, as the representatives of state power, sit wherever the light would be to their back so their faces would be obscured in shadow!

Fig. 16. Suggested alternatives for British judges' dress.
(Crown Copyright, Department for Constitutional Affairs.
Lord Chancellor's consultation paper, court working dress in
England and Wales, May 2003.)

Each of these modes of representation, like those of
Justice—sword and scales in hand, usually portrayed in
the West as a woman—also imply that the law is, like
culture itself, immanent, immune to human creation
and manipulation notwithstanding the efforts of the
shortsighted to the contrary. Blackstone, in the eighteenth century, could argue that just as certain mani-
festations (Shakespeare's incomparable writing, for example) could seem so right as to be a force of nature,
so too institutions that might seem to be of human cre-

ation fit so clearly with the unalterable features of God's own creations as to make laws themselves part of nature. Modern positivists, like Hart and Dworkin, see law as autonomous from the society in which it operates, such that truly correct answers by a right-minded adjudicator are not only possible but requisite. Indeed, as Boorstin has put it, "the rise of self-conscious lawmaking does not abolish the need for belief in immanence, it merely transforms that belief. It makes the need for that belief more acute." Or, as Stanley Fish has argued, "The law is continuously engaged in effacing the ideological content of its mechanisms so that it can present itself as a 'discourse which is context independent in its claims to universality and reason.'" To some this immanence argues for the retention or reintroduction of jury unanimity; to others it is embraced in the crosscutting roles of those impaneled to decide a dispute. Procedures, too, are highly ritualized, whether it is in the formalities of court etiquette or the regularities that inform a village gathering or mediational session.

Peter Brown has said that "an ambiguity lies at the heart of every ceremony," and there is as much truth in this for legal rituals as for any others. No legal proceeding can recapitulate exactly what happened: Even if a video replay is available (as in the notorious beating by Los Angeles police of Rodney King), others must interpret what they are seeing and what is present in each person's mind. Moreover, like all rituals, there is

Fig. 17. Images of justice (*above and opposite*). Portrayal of Justice, with scales and sword, beside Prudence, with mirror, unknown from the sixteenth century (see 9A Bartsch, *Le Peintre Graveur* 45 [Cor-Met, B.2, ed. 1970, reprint of 1920–22 Würzburg ed., reset of Leipzig, 1854–70], Warburg Institute, University of London.)

Parody of blindfolded justice. Albrecht Dürer, woodcut illus-
tration of Sebastian Brant's *Ship of Fools,* 1494. (Beinecke
Rare Book Collection, Yale University.)

Fig. 18. Cartoon about justice by Robert Mankoff. (© The New Yorker Magazine, 1981.)

uncertainty about making the transition from potentially destructive events to recapturing the order of the world. Many of the features of any ritual, therefore, have as part of their aim the restoration of a felt sense of order for which even rational elements of procedure and decision-making may have to take a back seat.

It is here that we can see how notions of justice and injustice may be played out in a legal context. Aristotle had distinguished between justice as following the letter of the law and justice as a form of equity, a realization that the particularities of instances may take precedence over uncritical uniformity. Was Creon right to insist on the letter of the law when he refused to allow the burial of Antigone's treasonous brother, or was he wrong to apply state law without considering the obligations of kinship? Without understanding the broader implications of justice in Greek culture its application in Greek law is, at best, incompletely appreciated. When, in the premodern West, justice was consonant with remaining true to positions established by tradition, the idea of justice had to change if the freedom of social movement and moral self-direction were to give birth to notions of equality. By contrast, in many contemporary religious communities and non-Western cultures, justice carries the implication not of equality but of equivalence, of fairness being achieved when the realities of difference by gender or role are given their proper due. Thus a woman may not be a priest in the Catholic Church or a rabbi in orthodox Judaism or an imam in Islam yet be regarded as fairly treated by virtue of the equivalent roles allotted to women in the family or other rituals. Notwithstanding H. L. Mencken's quip that "injustice is relatively easy to bear; what stings is justice," it is injustice that may be felt far more keenly than justice, as much because one's expectations of reciprocity have not been fulfilled as through the violation of some intangible ideal. In each instance, one cannot abstract "justice" from context, even though the law itself may give rather poor voice to its own criteria.

Consider, for example, some of those situations in which appellate courts in the United States have direct recourse to concepts of justice. In a number of cases involving consumers who were presented warranties that severely limited their claims against the manufacturer or seller, courts have drawn on the phrasing of earlier tribunals who spoke of "the demands of social justice" as a way of asserting both the changing nature of the marketplace and the purchasers' roles in it. In a U.S. Supreme Court decision involving child abuse and custody, to take another example, Justice Blackmun castigated the majority for their "sterile formalism" and said of his own approach to interpreting the Constitution in such a case: "I would adopt a 'sympathetic' reading, one which comports with dictates of fundamental justice and recognizes that compassion need not be exiled from the province of judging." Often dismissed as mere dicta or, worse yet, as rhetorical expressions of a dangerous, even antilegal, discretion, such phrasings tend to occur when the strict letter of the law seems to have been outstripped by social change, or when the moral nudge of an appeal to justice would seem to give voice to public sentiment, if not outrage. Others take a different tack. They may appeal to "natural law," which may mask personal morality or religious conviction, or reflect a philosophical penchant or historical claim. From the perspective of its critics, however, natural law exists only in the eye of the beholder or misses the point that, given the nature of our cultural creations, there is no such thing as natural law, only law naturalized.

Alternatively, someone like Justice Antonin Scalia, in a number of his U.S. Supreme Court opinions, says that fundamental constitutional rights should be lim-

ited to "an interest traditionally protected by our society . . . [ones] so rooted in the traditions and conscience of our people as to be ranked as fundamental."
He thus supports male-only military academies, even
though they receive state funds, claiming of one academy's code that none of us "will be better off for its destruction"—a code, incidentally, that provides, among
other strictures, that "a Gentleman does not hail a lady
from a club window, Does not mention names exactly
as he avoids the mention of what things cost, [and]
Does not slap strangers on the back nor so much as lay
a finger on a lady." It is difficult, however, to know how
long or how widely under this standard a practice must
exist to qualify as a "tradition," much less what objective
criteria can be applied for its discernment. Yet one may
equally ask whether such a standard does not articulate
more directly what others treat by avoidance or dissim-
ulation, namely the attempt to have the world make
sense by asserting who it is we think we are.

Indeed, the unarticulated but felt sense of order in
law may actually work its way into the very structure of
the legal system in a variety of ways. It has often been
said, for instance, that in establishing criminal laws we
proceed by making the punishment fit the crime. This
notion, sometimes called the Mikado principle from
its employment in the Gilbert and Sullivan song, was
phrased by Thomas Jefferson thus: "[I]t becomes a
duty in the legislature to arrange in a proper scale the
crimes which it may be necessary for them to repress,

and to adjust thereto a corresponding gradation of punishments." But in many historical instances one might argue that the exact opposite better describes the course of Western criminal law. That is, judges and juries have frequently found the punishment far too harsh for what is acknowledged to be some form of wrongdoing and, short of nullifying the law, they have created, or forced the creation, of a more differentiated set of crimes to accord with what they regard as an appropriate punishment. As Norman Douglas put it: "The law does not content itself with classifying and punishing crime. It invents crime." In a variant of this principle, it will be recalled, several Scandinavian courts have fined traffic offenders according to their income: Finnish police gave a $216,900 speeding ticket to a millionaire, based on his income tax information. Jurors have sometimes approached the issue of appropriate penalties by finding a defendant guilty of a lesser included offense when the evidence clearly supports the stronger verdict whose punishment they regard as too harsh. And federal judges in the United States revolted against mandatory sentences, though it remains to be seen whether the result will be a more refined set of crimes, rather than a more refined set of punishments.

The sense of incongruity between existing practice and changed circumstances may also account, in part, for procedural elements. Historically, lawyers and clients seeking remedies not recognized in law had to backtrack to the cause of action and then move forward again from a sense of injustice to a corresponding right. Where British and American law had institutionalized some of these changes through separate courts of equity, continental systems made their paradigm shifts, with greater or lesser success, through a sense of the morally awkward situation propelling claims to a higher law. In each instance, of course, a correlative shift in the very idea of justice—or at least renewed philosophical debate on the issue—flagged the need for recourse to a revised image of the sense of social order. Reasoning styles may play into these patterns: Cass Sunstein, for example, argues that analogic reasoning helps to avoid divisive social issues inasmuch as "incompletely theorized judgments" actually reinforce orderliness.

Another way of approaching the relation of the cosmic order to the strictly legal is that of the Chinese legalists of the nineteenth century to criminal law. They believed that one should not provide details of what is forbidden lest people assume that all other acts are permissible. As Lao-Tse said: The greater the number of statutes, the greater the number of thieves and brigands. It is an approach that tries to have it both ways—legal authority coupled with discouraging behavior that is socially dangerous or morally suspect. It fit quite nicely with a Confucian emphasis on legitimacy generally based on age and experience. Not surprisingly, this is the same mentality that informs many

university disciplinary systems, where the tension between a rule of law and the university *in loco parentis* is
often ill resolved.

If a legal system may, in part, serve to maintain the
cosmos, it is also significant to note when this emphasis
seems most vital. We have already seen that at moments of contested social change—in family matters or
in the idea of inner states—the propulsion to tie various cultural domains together may be intense. It may
also appear most strongly when the results or norms
of a given statutory structure no longer seem to satisfy
existing sensibilities. To take an example once again
from the field of family law: For a long time adoption
agencies sought to match children to adopting parents
on the basis of shared race or religion. There were always certain exceptions that seemed to prove an existing social rule: In the United States, for example,
whites who would never adopt a black child would ea-
gerly adopt a Native American, whether as part of a
kind of missionary mentality, moral ambivalence about
the historic treatment of Native Americans, or because, as yet another form of cultural cannibalism,
such boundary crossing in the heart of the family demonstrated the charity or triumph of the conqueror. But
when, in the years after the civil rights movement, attempts were made to separate children simply because
one parent was living with someone of another race or
in a minority neighborhood, the propulsion to recon-
figure relationships in a way that could suit new sensi-

bilities became unavoidable. The result was that a set
of cultural categories that seemed more comprehensive and hence orderly, even if it did not accord with
everyone's values, took hold, yielding a way in which
people could get on with their lives. Making everyday
sense may, at times, trump almost any other social and
personal need.

To a number of recent legal philosophers, however,
such assertions mask the actual dynamics of power.
Whether as part of the critical legal studies movement
or from the perspective of critical race or feminist theory, their arguments, as we have seen, center on the
proposition that beneath assertedly neutral principles
of law lurks the distribution of power that has, particularly in the West, favored men, the rich, or the well
connected. At one level such analyses are unexcep-
tional: Who can doubt that those who are more favor-
ably positioned to pass legislation or afford expensive
legal counsel or sustain costly litigation are not in a
better position to have their way? And one does not
have to favor a Marxist view of the law to suspect that
the superstructure of legal propositions and institutions is deeply entwined with those whose access to resources places them in an advantageous competitive
position. But it is just as clear that this is not the whole
story, that many precepts are sufficiently shared across
internal divisions so as to be comprehensible and acceptable to people not just because they have been so-
ciologically brainwashed but because they find the

world comprehensible in these terms. The failure to take seriously people's cultural concepts as part of their chosen world, and not simply as one imposed upon them, can distort the role of law in their lives every bit as much as failing to consider how their choices may be limited.

Indeed, new normative communities are constantly being formed. The legal development of the European Community and of international law generally may suggest that new legal hybrids are developing. But this is by no means a necessary consequence of greater economic and political involvement. Sometimes it is the law of one jurisdiction that becomes all but universally accepted: International contract law, for example, is increasingly controlled, through the choice of the parties, by the law of either Britain or New York State. In other instances changes are the price of greater international involvement: As a condition for possible inclusion in the European Union, Turkey has had to abolish the death penalty and create new courts to deal with intellectual property, consumer issues, juveniles, and family law—a process that has led one Turkish bar association president to comment that "nowhere in the world have so many laws that affect you from the day you are born until the day you die, been passed in such a rush." Some aspects of the law of the Internet are, indeed, bringing Asian and Western countries together for commercial reasons, even though they may have quite different political interests in the control of what can go out over the network. In Britain, however, the expectation by some—the fear by others—that the European Convention on Human Rights would take the place of the country's unwritten constitution has proved illusory: Few cases turn on claims under the Convention, the common law having accommodated many changes in its own terms. Sometimes reference to other nations' laws is actually mandated: The courts of South Africa, for example, are obliged, in certain kinds of similar cases, to consider the decisions of other jurisdictions, while a number of European courts—but very few American courts—cite other countries' approaches with increasing frequency.

Local concepts of law and their political contexts will not necessarily merge effortlessly. Sharp differences exist, for instance, in the idea of what can be "owned" when dealing with intellectual "property." And British ideas of private law and European notions of public law are not a perfect match. Nor can one ever discount the extent to which national laws are central to national identity. Claire Booth Luce, as long ago as 1943, referred to globalism as "globaloney." The human propensity to differentiate categories of experience suggests that one ignores the local at one's peril, and it may be that it is in the law that the contest between a sense of the local and the global will receive some of its most serious testing.

Conclusion

A lawyer who has not studied economics and sociology is very apt to become a public enemy.
—Justice Louis Brandeis, 1916

A great deal of ink has been spilled over the years trying to define law, but characterizing law simply as ordered relations has several advantages. For one, we can see that it is an active process that affects the way people orient themselves towards one another's actions, and that this is accomplished, like all other aspects of culture, through the process of creating categories of experience and weaving them into a distinctive configuration. Without either reifying law or rendering it the mere justification of the powerful, such an approach also suggests lines of inquiry and forms of practical application that are worthy of note.

By seeing law as culture some of the myths of immanence may be replaced by a perfectly legitimate argument that, as Michael Walzer has put it, something may or may not be right in an absolute sense but it can be assessed in terms of whether it is right *for us*. That fit of legal sensibility and cultural style will take place whether we try to ignore it or not, and it is by grasping the very nature of culture and law's place within it— grasping the symbiotic relation of a culture's constituent domains and the ways in which they are interlaced—that the place of law in the ordering of relationships may most realistically be sought. Indeed, the comparison of legal systems suggests that conflict is neither the inescapable norm of human relationships nor the sole focus for the mechanisms generated by them. Grasping the world, attending to the potential sources of discomfort, and introducing an outside voice to relations that require attention rank as high in legal systems as do the rules and procedures for addressing conflict. And if comparison reveals possibilities of relationship, if seeking unrecognized connections heightens the awareness of who we are, or if the quest for the meaning of one's universe through the regularities of one's life reveals the plasticity of our social and cultural forms, the result can only be a fuller sense of what it means to be human.

Law in this sense never stands apart from life—some refined essence of professional inquiry or arcane speech. Rather, it forms the conscious attention we give to our relationships. Like art and literature, through law we attempt to order our ties to one another. Like religion and ritual it may be a cloak for self-interest; like commerce and politics it may lay claim to justifications in nature or universal morality. However it is displayed, however it is applied, we can no more comprehend the roles of legal institutions without seeing them as part of their culture than we can fully understand each culture without attending to its form of law. In the end, it may be worthwhile, then, to think of law as universal in this one sense—as a marvelous entry to the study of that most central of human features, culture itself, and hence an open invitation, whatever one's ultimate interests, to thinking about what and who we are.

Further Reading

The literature on law and culture is, of course, vast. Studies of their relation, however, are often at their best when they are about particular societies and times, rather than abstract accounts or universalizing claims, or when they cross disciplinary boundaries to show the integration of a culture. The readings mentioned here are, therefore, keyed to the issues raised in the text and are offered as examples of readable and insightful studies that blend theory and circumstance to great effect.

Frontispiece

The full English text on the candle reads as follows:

God is our refuge and strength.

Dear Lord, say unto the judge to stand beside me and make war against my enemies who threaten to spill my life's blood.

Dear God intercede for me. Bring me peace and comfort—and let me breathe the air of freedom.

Amen

Anoint with court oil.
Burn John Conqueror incense.

Write your hope and desire.

Preface

Clifford Geertz's application of cultural analysis to law, in the title essay of his *Local Knowledge* (New York: Basic Books, 1983), is a valuable starting point for further reading. The quotation is from that text at 182.

Introduction

The Muddarubba case, initially reported in *Northern Territories Journal* 317 (1951–76), and a set of related materials are reprinted in Joseph Goldstein, Alan M. Dershowitz, and Richard D. Schwartz, *Criminal Law: Theory and Process*, 2nd ed. (New York: Free Press, 1974). For a description of other cultural defense cases, see Alison Dundes Renteln, *The Cultural Defense* (New York: Oxford University Press, 2004). The post-Nazi German case and supplementary materials will be found in Rudolph B. Schlesinger, *Comparative Law* (Mineola, N.Y.: Foundation Press, 1988); the anecdote about the lonely Japanese man is in Joel Rosch, "Institutionalizing Mediation: The Evolution of the Civil Liberties Bureau in Japan," *Law and Society Review* 21, no. 2 (1987): 243–66. The best introduction to the anthropological theory of culture remains Clifford Geertz's *The Interpretation of Cultures* (New York: Basic Books 1973). The quote by him is from "Off Echoes," *Political and Legal Anthropology Review* 19, no. 2 (1996): 35. The quotation by Edward Levi is from an occasional paper published by the Law School of the University of Chicago, called "An Approach to Law," at 4.

Chapter 1: Law and Social Control

Stewart Macaulay's original essay is "Non-Contractual Relations in Business," *American Sociological Review* 28, no. 1 (1963): 55–

67. He has updated and expanded his analysis many times in the years since: For recent overviews see "The Real and the Paper Deal: Empirical Pictures of Relationships, Complexity and the Urge for Transparent Simple Rules," *Modern Law Review* 66, no. 1 (2003): 44–79; and "Freedom From Contract: Solutions in Search of a Problem?" *Wisconsin Law Review* 2004, no. 2: 777–820. The classic anthropological account of gossip remains Max Gluckman, "Gossip and Scandal," *Current Anthropology* 4, no. 3 (1963): 307–16; Pamela J. Stewart and Andrew Strathern, *Witchcraft, Sorcery, Rumors, and Gossip* (New York: Cambridge University Press, 2004), offer an overview of the theories and practices associated with these forms of social control. The quotation by Elizabeth Colson is from "The Contentiousness of Disputes," in *Understanding Disputes: The Politics of Argument*, ed. Pat Caplan (Oxford: Berg, 1995), 65–82, at 80. The quotation about law and reality is from Peter Fitzpatrick, "Law and Societies," *Osgoode Hall Law Journal* 22 (1984): 115–38, at 127.

Max Gluckman's *The Judicial Process among the Barotse of Northern Rhodesia* (Manchester: Manchester University Press, 1955) contains numerous cases demonstrating the limits of judicial power in relation to crosscutting relationships. Lewis Coser's *The Functions of Social Conflict* (New York: Free Press, 1956) counters the view that all conflict is dysfunctional. Stuart Schlegel's *Tiruray Justice* (Berkeley and Los Angeles: University of California Press, 1970), which applies the theories in H.L.A. Hart's *The Concept of Law* (Oxford: Clarendon Press, 1961) to a Philippine society, is an exemplary account of an indigenous legal/moral system.

Litigation involving Jehovah's Witnesses has contributed greatly to American First Amendment law: The case involving Judge Wright is "Application of the President and Directors of Georgetown College, Inc.," *Federal Reporter, Second Series* 331 (D.C. Circuit Court 1964), 1000–1010. The incident involving

the Dalkon Shield is discussed in Sheldon Engelmayer and Robert Wagman, *Lord's Justice* (New York: Doubleday, 1985). The
quote about Karl Llewellyn is from Allen R. Kamp, "Downtown
Code: A History of the Uniform Commercial Code, 1949–
1954," *Buffalo Law Review* 49 (2001): 359–476, at 392.

Mixed juries in early England are discussed in Marianne Con-
stable, *The Law of the Other* (Chicago: University of Chicago Press
1991). Lauren Benton's *Law and Colonial Cultures* (Cambridge:
Cambridge University Press, 2002) is an excellent overview of
that subject. Julie Stewart's "Why I Can't Teach Customary
Law," in *The Changing Family*, ed. John Eekelaar and Thanda-
bantu Nhlapo (Oxford: Hart, 1998), 217–29, at 219, is the
source for the quote about customary law in Zimbabwe; for the
quote on custom taking precedence over Islamic law, see Haim
Gerber, *Islamic Law and Culture, 1600–1840* (Leiden: Brill,
1999), 105.

For a fascinating analysis of the dearth of public control in
the ancient world, see Virginia Hunter, *Policing Athens: Social
Control in the Attic Lawsuits, 420–320 B.C.* (Princeton: Princeton
University Press, 1994). Lisa Bernstein, "Opting Out of the
Legal System: Extralegal Contractual Relations in the Diamond Industry," *Journal of Legal Studies* 21, no. 1 (1992): 115–
57, is one of several studies she has made of social control in
a given trade.

For the development of the idea of unconscionability, see
Ajay K. Mehrota, "Law and the 'Other': Karl N. Llewellyn, Cultural Anthropology, and the Legacy of *The Cheyenne Way*," *Law
and Social Inquiry* 26 (2001): 741–72. The argument that Llewellyn drew the idea of unconscionability from his experience
studying the Cheyenne is alluded to in William Twining, *Karl
Llewellyn and the Realist Movement* (London: Weidenfeld and Nic-
olson, 1973). On the preference for procedural over substantive justice, see E. Allen Lind and Tom R. Tyler, *The Social Psy-*

chology of Procedural Justice (New York: Plenum Press, 1988). On the uses and avoidance of law in small-town America, see Carol J. Greenhouse, Barbara Yngvesson, and David M. Engel, *Law and Community in Three American Towns* (Ithaca: Cornell University Press, 1994).

For a study of Islamic law and society, see my book *The Anthropology of Justice: Law as Culture in Islamic Society* (Cambridge: Cambridge University Press, 1989). Japanese society and law has been the subject of many studies. Chie Nakane's *Japanese Society* (Berkeley and Los Angeles: University of California Press, 1970) is still one of the best, along with Robert J. Smith, *Japanese Society* (Cambridge: Cambridge University Press, 1983), and the legal study by V. Lee Hamilton and Joseph Sanders, *Everyday Justice: Responsibility and the Individual in Japan and the United States* (New Haven: Yale University Press, 1992). The African example is from James L. Gibbs, Jr., "The Kpelle Moot: A Therapeutic Model for the Informal Settlement of Disputes," *Africa* 33 (1963): 1–11. The Jewish Conciliation Board is described in James Yaffe, *So Sue Me: The Story of a Community Court* (New York: Saturday Review Press, 1972). Yaffe's account has been supplemented here thanks to visits to the board over the years by some of my students.

On legal taxonomies see the essay entitled "Islamic Law as Common Law: Power, Culture, and the Reconfiguration of Legal Taxonomies" in my book, *The Justice of Islam* (Oxford: Oxford University Press 2000), 38–68. Among many fine studies of law in context are John Comaroff and Simon Roberts, *Rules and Processes: The Cultural Logic of Dispute in an African Context* (Chicago: University of Chicago Press, 1981); Lloyd A. Fallers, *Law Without Precedent: Legal Ideas in Action in the Courts of Colonial Busoga* (Chicago: University of Chicago Press, 1969); and Sally Falk Moore, *Law as Process* (London: Routledge and Kegan Paul, 1978). For excellent descriptions of European and Soviet

trials, see Sybille Bedford, *The Faces of Justice* (New York: Simon
and Schuster, 1961); and George Feifer, *Justice in Moscow* (New
York: Simon and Schuster, 1964).

Chapter 2: Creating Facts

The quotation and analysis of Cretan oaths is from Michael
Herzfeld, "Pride and Perjury: Time and the Oath in the Moun-
tain Villages of Crete," *Man*, n.s. 25, no. 2 (1990): 305–20.

Of the many studies on the history of the jury the following
are useful introductions: Leonard W. Levy, *The Palladium of Jus-
tice: Origins of Trial by Jury* (Chicago: Ivan R. Dee, 1999); Thomas
Andrew Green, *Verdict According to Conscience: Perspectives on the
English Criminal Trial Jury, 1200–1800* (Chicago: University of
Chicago Press, 1985); and Norman F. Cantor, *The English* (New
York: Simon and Schuster, 1967). The instruction to English
jurors following the abolition of the oath, together with a description of the period generally, will be found at p. 187 of
Danny Danziger and John Gillingham, *1215: The Year of Magna
Carta* (New York: Simon and Schuster, 2003). On the changes
in medieval rituals, including ordeals, see Peter Brown, "Society
and the Supernatural: A Medieval Change," *Daedalus* 104, no.
2 (1975): 133–51. On the persistance of duels and blood feuds
after the Conquest, see Paul R. Hyams, *Rancor and Reconciliation
in Medieval England* (Ithaca: Cornell University Press, 2003).

Useful online sites for original documents on medieval law
include The Internet Medieval Sourcebook, Medieval Legal
History (www.fordham.edu/halsall/sbook-law.html); and the
Avalon Project at the Yale Law School Library (www.yale.edu/
library/).

For a defense of the jury and its powers of nullification, see
Jeffrey Abrahamson, *We, The Jury: The Jury System and the Ideal of
Democracy* (New York: Basic Books, 1994). For studies of jury

decision-making, see Reid Hastie, Steven D. Penrod, and Nancy Pennington, *Inside the Jury* (Cambridge: Harvard University Press, 1983). For a series of comparisons of the jury in various parts of the world, see the special issue of *Law and Contemporary Problems* 62 (1999); Neil Vidmar, ed., *World Jury Systems* (Oxford: Oxford University Press, 2000); and Roderick Mundy, "What do the French Think of their Jury? Views from Poitiers and Paris," *Legal Studies* 15 (1995): 65–87.

For the example of an American court equating the utterance of the word *bullshit* with silence, see People v. Nitti, *Illinois Reporter* 312, 73–99 (also *Northeast Reporter* 143, 448–57) (Supreme Court of Illinois, 1924).

On the rise of the concept of the individual, see Colin Morris, *The Discovery of the Individual, 1050–1200* (New York: Harper and Row, 1972). Morris's views have been debated and revised in Caroline Walker Bynum, "Did the Twelfth Century Discover the Individual?" in *Jesus as Mother: Studies in the Spirituality of the High Middle Ages* (Berkeley and Los Angeles: University of California Press, 1982); John F. Benton, "Individualism and Conformity in Medieval Western Europe," in *Individualism and Conformity in Classical Islam*, ed. Amin Benani and Speros Vryonis (Wiesbaden: Otto Harrassowitz, 1977), 145–58, and Colin Morris, "Individualism in Twelfth-Century Religion: Some Further Reflections," *Journal of Ecclesiastical History* 31 (1980): 195–206. On the fragmentation of the self, particularly as it relates to Peter Abelard's thought, see the chapter entitled "The Invention and Fission of the Public Persona," in Arno Borst, *Medieval Worlds* (Chicago: University of Chicago Press, 1992); and Chris D. Ferguson, "Autobiography as Therapy: Guibert de Nogent, Peter Abelard, and the Making of Medieval Autobiography," *Journal of Medieval and Renaissance Studies* 13, no. 2 (1983): 187–212. See generally, Georges Duby and Philippe Braunstein, "The Emergence of the Individual," in *A His-*

tory of the Private Life, ed. Georges Duby, vol. 2, *Representations of the Medieval World* (Cambridge: Harvard University Press, 1988), 507–630. R. Howard Bloch's *Medieval French Literature and Law* (Berkeley and Los Angeles: University of California Press, 1977) is also an insightful study of how law and culture changed in relation to one another in this period, while the choice of legal forums is analyzed in Daniel Lord Smail, *The Consumption of Justice: Emotion, Publicity, and Legal Culture in Marseilles, 1264–1423* (Ithaca: Cornell University Press, 2003).

For the development of probability in the West, see Ian Hacking, *The Emergence of Probability* (Cambridge: Cambridge University Press, 1975); and Barbara J. Shapiro, *Probability and Certainty in Seventeenth-Century England* (Princeton: Princeton University Press, 1983), (from which the quote is derived at p. 272). The quote by Justice Ginsburg is from Victor v. Nebraska, *United States Reports* 511 (1994) 1–38, at 23.

For a comparative and evolutionary view of law and morality as represented in literature, see Theodore Ziolkowski, *The Mirror of Justice* (Princeton: Princeton University Press, 1997). For background on many famous cases, see John T. Noonan, *Persons and Masks of the Law* (Berkeley and Los Angeles: University of California Press, 2002); and A. W. Brian Simpson, *Leading Cases in the Common Law* (Oxford: Clarendon Press, 1995). The legal effects of the speech styles of women and minorities are explored in William M. O'Barr, *Linguistic Evidence: Language, Power, and Strategy in the Courtroom* (New York: Academic Press, 1982). The cultural context of sentencing is analyzed in Stanton Wheeler, Kenneth Mann, and Austin Sarat, *Sitting in Judgment: The Sentencing of White-Collar Offenders* (New Haven: Yale University Press, 1988).

A broad comparison of legal systems will be found in H. Patrick Glenn, *Legal Traditions of the World* (Oxford: Oxford University Press, 2000), from which the cited passage is at 216. The quotation from Jacob Neusner is from his overview of Jewish legal thought, *Judaism: The Evidence of the Mishnah* (Chicago: University of Chicago Press, 1981), 282. The pornography cases are Shaw v. Director of Public Prosecutions (1961), 2 *All England Reports* 446, while the famous statement about knowing pornography when he sees it appears in Justice Potter Stewart's concurring opinion in Jacobellis v. Ohio, *United States Reports* 378 (1964), 184–204, at 197.

Kenneth Clark's doll tests—which purported to show that 52 percent of black children in the South (and 69 percent of those in the North) thought the white doll was "nice," while 49 percent of black children in the South (and 71 percent of those in the North) characterized the black doll as "bad"—has been much criticized. See the profile of Dr. Kenneth Clark by Nat Hentoff in the *New Yorker*, August 23, 1982, 37–73. Distinguishing science from "junk science" is discussed in Sheila Jasanoff, *Science at the Bar: Law, Science, and Technology in America* (Cambridge: Harvard University Press, 1995). On the role of experts in choosing jurors, see Shari Seidman Diamond, "Scientific Jury Selection: What Social Scientists Know and Do Not Know," *Judicature* 73, no. 4 (1990): 178–83; and Jeremy W. Barber, "The Jury is Still Out: The Role of Jury Science in the Modern American Courtroom," *American Criminal Law Review* 31, no. 4 (1994): 1225–52.

Chapter 3: Reason, Power, Law

Richard Posner's comment on legal reasoning is from his *Overcoming Law* (Cambridge: Harvard University Press, 1995), 188. For a polemic against the arcane claims of legal reasoning, see Paul F. Campos, *Jurismania: The Madness of American Law* (New York: Oxford University Press, 1998).

The classic study of the jury is Harry Kalven, Jr. and Hans Zeisel, *The American Jury* (Boston: Little, Brown, 1966).

On metaphor, see Susan Sontag, *Illness as Metaphor and AIDS and its Metaphors* (New York: Anchor, 1990); Mark Rose, "Copyright and its Metaphors," *UCLA Law Review* 50, no. 1 (2002): 1–15; and Emily Martin, "The Egg and the Sperm," *Signs* 16, no. 3 (1991): 485–501.

The indispensable starting point for a study of common-law legal reasoning is Edward H. Levi, *An Introduction to Legal Reasoning* (Chicago: University of Chicago Press, 1949). The ways in which courts tell the stories about people and legal categories is the subject of Anthony G. Amsterdam and Jerome Bruner, *Minding the Story* (Cambridge: Harvard University Press, 2000). On character evidence, see H. Richard Uviller, "Evidence of Character to Prove Conduct: Illusion, Illogic, and Injustice in the Courtroom," *University of Pennsylvania Law Review* 130 (1982): 845–91. The statement that "we can tolerate the justice in factual ambiguity" is from Richard K. Sherwin, "Law Frames: Historical Truth and Narrative Necessity in a Criminal Case," *Stanford Law Review* 47 (1994): 39–83, at 77.

For a review of the arguments about the history of jury nullification, see Simon Stern, "Between Local Knowledge and National Politics: Debating Rationales for Jury Nullification after Bushell's Case," *Yale Law Journal* 111, no. 7 (2002): 1815–60; and Nancy S. Marder, "The Myth of Jury Nullification," *Northwestern Law Review*, vol. 93, no. 3 (1999): 877–959.

For a study of the British use of the repugnancy clause, see Zaki Mustafa, *Common Law in the Sudan: An Account of the "Justice, Equity, and Good Conscience" Provision* (Oxford: Clarendon Press, 1971).

For a symbolic interaction approach to capturing the terms of a situation, see Peter McHugh, *Defining the Situation: The Organization of Meaning in Social Interaction* (Indianapolis: Bobbs-Merrill, 1968).

Chapter 4: Law as Cosmology

On the history of kleptomania, see Elaine S. Abelson, *When La-dies Go A-Thieving: Middle Class Shoplifters in the Victorian Depart-ment Store* (Oxford: Oxford University Press, 1989). On psycho-logical parenthood, the key source is Joseph Goldstein, Anna Freud, and Albert J. Solnit, *Beyond the Best Interests of the Child* (New York: Free Press, 1973). Injustice is the focus of Judith N. Shklar, *The Faces of Injustice* (New Haven: Yale University Press, 1990). Representations of justice are discussed in Dennis E. Curtis and Judith Resnick, "Images of Justice," *Yale Law Journal* 96, no. 8 (1987): 1727–72. The quotation by V. C. Igbokwe is from "Some Socio-Cultural Dimensions of Dispute Resolution: Informal Justice Processes among Ibo-Speaking Peoples of East-ern Nigeria and their Implications for Community/Neighbour-ing Justice System in North America," *African Journal of Interna-tional and Comparative Law* 10, no. 3 (1998): 446–71, at 455. For the Tibetan example of law as cosmology, see Rebecca French, *The Golden Yoke: The Legal Cosmology of Buddhist Tibet* (Ithaca: Cornell University Press, 1995).

On the questionable nature of eyewitness testimony and its expert presentation, see Elizabeth F. Loftus, "Ten Years in the Life of an Expert Witness," *Law and Human Behavior* 10, no. 3 (1986): 241–63, and her *Eyewitness Testimony* (Cambridge: Har-vard University Press, 1979). For the anthropologists' involve-ment in Indian Claims Commission proceedings, see the spe-cial issue "Anthropology and Indian Claims Litigation," *Ethnohistory* 2 (1955). The quote on cultural fiction is from Campos, *Jurismania*, 121.

The 1974 case of African scarification, Regina v. Adesanya, though unreported, is discussed in Sebastian Poulter, *English Law and Ethnic Minority Customs* (London: Butterworths, 1986), 151. On the potential mismatch between British private law and Continental public law, see J.W.F. Allison, *A Continental Distinc-*

tion in Common Law: A Historical and Comparative Perspective on English Public Law (Oxford: Clarendon Press, 1996). For a distinctive interpretation of the controversy about the effects of female genital mutilation, see Richard A. Schweder, *Why Do Men Barbecue? Recipes for Cultural Psychology* (Cambridge: Harvard University Press, 2003), 168–216.

Index

Printed in the USA
CPSIA information can be obtained
at www.ICGtesting.com
JSHW081409110823
46409JS00003B/9

9 780691 136448